Gaming the system

FINANCIAL TIMES
Prentice Hall

In an increasingly competitive world, it is quality
of thinking that gives an edge – an idea that opens new
doors, a technique that solves a problem, or an insight
that simply helps make sense of it all.

We work with leading authors in the fields of
management and finance to bring cutting-edge thinking
and best learning practice to a global market.

Under a range of leading imprints, including
Financial Times Prentice Hall, we create world-class
print publications and electronic products giving
readers knowledge and understanding which can then
be applied, whether studying or at work.

To find out more about our business and professional
products, you can visit us at www.business-minds.com

For other Pearson Education publications, visit
www.pearsoned-ema.com

Pearson
Education

Gaming the system

How to stop playing the organizational game, and start playing the competitive game

James B. Rieley

FINANCIAL TIMES

Prentice Hall

London ● New York ● San Francisco ● Toronto ● Sydney ● Tokyo ● Singapore
Hong Kong ● Cape Town ● Madrid ● Paris ● Milan ● Munich ● Amsterdam

PEARSON EDUCATION LIMITED

Head Office:
Edinburgh Gate
Harlow CM20 2JE
Tel: +44 (0)1279 623623
Fax: +44 (0)1279 431059

London Office:
128 Long Acre, London WC2E 9AN
Tel: +44 (0)20 7447 2000
Fax: +44 (0)20 7240 5771
Website: www.business-minds.com

First published in Great Britain in 2001

ISBN 0 273 65419 5

British Library Cataloguing in Publication Data
A CIP catalogue record for this book can be obtained from the British Library.

The title of Chapter 3, *I change by not changing at all*, is a lyric from
"Elderly Woman Behind the Counter in a Small Town," Pearl Jam, 1993.

10 9 8 7 6 5 4

Typeset by Northern Phototypesetting Co. Ltd, Bolton
Printed and bound in Great Britain by Biddles Ltd, Guildford & King's Lynn

The Publishers' policy is to use paper manufactured from sustainable forests.

About the author

James B. Rieley is the Global Head of Leadership Development for Celerant Consulting. Rieley, who has a doctorate degree in Organizational Effectiveness, additionally has a B.S. in Business Administration, and was the president of a successful plastics manufacturing company for more than 20 years. After selling his company in 1987, he began to work with organizations in the area of innovation and organizational dynamics. He lives in London.

He has written extensively on the subject of quality, having been published in *Journal of Organizational Excellence*, *National Productivity Review*, *The Systems Thinker*, *The Business Journal*, *Quality Progress*, *Leverage*, *On The Horizon*, *Community College Journal*, *Corporate Reports Wisconsin*, and other publications. He is the author of a research report for GOAL/QPC on strategic planning for education, entitled *Closing the Loop*, and co-author of an implementation workbook on *Institutional Effectiveness*. His work has been cited in *Fast Company*, *Making It Happen: Stories from Inside the New Workplace*, *A Fieldguide for Focused Planning*, and *Breakthrough Leadership*.

Rieley is certified by the Covey Leadership Center in the Seven Habits of Highly Effective People; he is the past President of Milwaukee: First in Quality, a network service of the Metropolitan Milwaukee Association of Commerce, a member of the Society for Organizational Learning, and the founder of the Southeast Wisconsin Organizational Learning Consortium (SEWOLC).

Contents

Acknowledgements

This book is the outcome of research into what helps to create and sustain organizational effectiveness. Although I will not be able to mention every person who has contributed to and supported my work, I would like to specifically mention my wife Mary Lee, whose love and support has made this project both possible and productive.

I would also like to thank Daniel Kim, whose work has been an inspiration to me and whose assistance has been invaluable in the development of this book; Jack Rieley, and Jaye Muller, for their continual support and encouragement; Sam Israelit, and John Birkholz, friends and associates, who have helped to create the environment that has enabled me to continue my process of learning and sharing and realizing my potential through my work; members of the MATC STOL Group, the Houston AABC Organizational Learning Group, and the CMC Leadership Development Team, who have helped to create and support practice fields for testing my assumptions and validating my work; MaryAnn Fusco and Janice Molloy, editors of *National Productivity Review* and *The Systems Thinker*, who have published some of the findings of this work in their publications over the past several years.

And finally my children, Matthew, David, Jeff, and Melissa, for whom I do this work so that their future working environments might become better places that can enable them to realize their personal potential.

Preface

Several years ago, I attended a workshop at which Robert Hanig talked about attitudes that people bring with them in similar situations. It struck me at the time that the attitudes he was talking about were the baggage that we all carry with us. Some of us, to paraphrase Hanig, come as vacationers – people who would rather attend the workshop than be in their normal, day-to-day jobs. Some come as sophisticates – people who have seen everything, know everything, and would probably participate on a physical basis only. Some would be there as prisoners – people who were instructed to attend, and probably instructed to learn as well. But then, Hanig said that some would also come as explorers – people who are seeking to learn more about something they already know a little about, or people who are seeking to learn about some of the things that they never even knew they didn't know. This book is all about exploring.

Change is something that we have no choice about. Change happens every minute of every day. Change is not bad; it is merely the essence of what we are all about as humans. From the moment we are conceived, we are undergoing change. We are born, we grow, we learn, we grow some more, we apply what we learn, we grow older, and then, well, we all know what happens next. We do not have any option other than to change, and to deal with the changes that we are faced with to the best of our ability.

> ● The changes that we experience directly, the changes in ourselves, are perhaps too close for us to realize on a day-to-day basis.

However, dealing with changes in our organizations tends to be not as easy for us. This could be for a variety of reasons.

The changes that we experience directly, the changes in ourselves, are perhaps too close for us to realize on a day-to-day basis. As we get older, we rarely see the changes until we compare who we have become with who we were. This is relatively easy to do – we look at photos of the past and compare them to who we are now. That enables us to see the difference, the change we have experienced. But seeing the changes as they happen is harder. We rarely notice the changes our bodies experience unless the change is dramatic – we don't notice our heart beating until it begins to beat incredibly fast; we don't notice our breathing until we are out of breath; we don't notice our growth until our clothes don't fit as well.

We experience changes in our organizational life as well. Many of these changes are not readily visible as they happen either. But sometimes, the change can seem very dramatic – our organizations are reorganized due to a merger, our organizations change due to advances in technology, our organizations change due to external forces that seem out of our control. When these changes happen, we can be mystified as to how to cope with them. This book will explore how, by focussing on how to enable change, we can become more adept at dealing with its effects on our organizations, and on ourselves.

This book is meant to be an exploration – an exploration of how we arrived at where we are, and why, and an exploration of how to move our organizations to where they want to be.

JBR

Introduction

How many times have you seen changes happen in your organization – changes that impact your ability to do what you believe you are supposed to do? How many times have you noticed that the messages that you receive within your company about what to do are seemingly at odds with the messages you previously received? How many times have you felt that the management of your company knows less about what you should do in your job than you do? When these things happen – when the world you work in changes to the point that it seems so disjointed you feel you need to do what you think is better – what happens? What happens is something called "gaming the system." Gaming the system is something that we all do, to a degree. But when many people in a company begin to "game the system," the long-term potential of the organization to be really successful, to realize its potential, is diminished.

Gaming the system is based on research I have conducted over the past ten years – research into why people in organizations act as they do. This does not mean that they are either good or bad; they simply demonstrate organizational behaviors as a result of certain dynamics at play. Over this period, I have conducted interviews with employees to explore some of the dynamics at play in the subject organizations.

This book is about those dynamics – how people's behaviors are changed due to the structures organizations put into place. The structures that are identified in this book are not physical – they are not buildings or facilities. The structures I talk about in *Gaming the system* are the policies and procedures, the mental models, and the stated goals that organizations put into place. It is these structures that drive people's behaviors, that I have identified here, that have dramatically changed the ability of the companies I have written about to become successful, or to be more successful. *Gaming the system* is about how people in companies shift their behaviors to deal with those structures.

Examples of gaming the system abound, and we all know what they are. In the past, we have simply not been able to identify the overall behavioral dynamic by name – until now. Gaming the system is rewarding those who are recognized to be good at firefighting instead of those who ensure that a company doesn't have the fires to fight. It is shifting the burden of effort (and blame) to avoid any potential consequences. It is avoiding accountability by keeping things "stirred up" in a company. It is manipulating an incentive system for personal gain. It is focussing on short-term thinking to avoid the responsibility of the future. And it is hiding or manipulating data.

> ● Gaming the system is a destructive personal and organizational behavior that saps the willingness and ability of those who want their companies to become successful.

Gaming the system is a destructive personal and organizational behavior that saps the willingness and ability of those who want their companies to become successful, sustainable, and rewarding environments in which we all would like to work.

By understanding how people game the system, and for what reasons, it is possible to slow down or reverse the impact of it, which is a benefit to both the people impacted by it, and the organization as a whole. But here is a cautionary note: if you believe that it is someone else's responsibility to make this happen, you are sadly mistaken. Throughout *Gaming the system* you will find examples of how and why the companies I have written about arrived at the place they have found themselves. And in each case, these dynamics could have been reversed by better understanding of what was going on, why it was going on, and what effect it would have on the people and the organization as a whole.

The book is divided into chapters, each representing the dynamics of an organization. In this process, I have captured many of the comments of the specific employees, and in many cases have inserted quotations from these people. I have used the quotations – from those who are experiencing the dynamics – to enable the reader to "feel" what the employees are feeling.

I have, for the purposes of retaining confidentiality, renamed the organizations in each of the chapters. By using a pseudonym for a company name, the reader can "stay with the flow" of the book, and be a part of what the organization is going through. At the end of each chapter, I have "retold" the story of the dynamics at play in the organization. This is then followed by conclusions that I have drawn from the intended, and unintended, consequences of those dynamics.

At the end of the book, I have offered suggestions for the reader. My experience has taught me that the dynamics at play in the subject organizations are dynamics that many organizations are experiencing. For a reader who can associate with those dynamics – and many of you will – it can be helpful to find ways of dealing with them, without having to reinvent every single potential wheel.

1

It is like driving at night, through the woods, in the fog, on a winding road, with no headlights

How we will be able to ensure our company's success

It has been said that it is almost impossible to get to where you want to go if you don't know where that place is. Many times, management of companies decide to set goals that are supposed to result in hoped-for benefits. On the surface, that seems like a good idea – set a goal, challenge the employees to meet it, get the payoff. But in many cases it doesn't work. What causes this inability to achieve company goals? The business journals abound with stories of missed goals, of efforts that have gone wide of their targets. Why is this?

In most cases, it is not from lack of effort but from lack of ability to clearly understand what the goals and targets are, and how they apply to the people in the company. Without having an understanding of what to do and for what reason, working might be like the title of this chapter, "it is like driving at night, through the woods, in the fog, on a winding road, with no headlights." And then we wonder why we can't get there.

ToolCo is not a real company, well, the name is not real. However, the people who work at ToolCo are real, and what they have been going through is real as well. ToolCo is an organization with a long history in the Midwest of the United States, and with a long-standing reputation for product excellence and innovation throughout the world. ToolCo is part of a larger company that has undergone many ownership changes in the past ten years, and was experiencing the pains of competition and a perceived lack of ability to realize its potential.

ToolCo has undergone tremendous change in its history. As a division of a larger holding company, it was initially a manufacturing division that built a reputation for excellence in its field of expertise – conveying equipment. Throughout the many changes in the parent company – an internal buyout, a takeover by a hostile suitor, and a sale to a substantially larger international conglomerate – it endured. But at a price. The ToolCo of today is not the ToolCo of the past. Some of the employees in the division have experienced many of these changes, and this had been reflected in their relative ability or inability to become emotionally involved in the organizational current state.

"The greatest barrier to becoming more effective? It's the willingness of the people to come together and work toward the future vs. protecting their territory."

"The biggest barrier to being the best? It's a management problem. It is our unwillingness, I think, to act."

Both these comments surfaced during employee interviews and are related to the culture of the organization. Culture has been defined by Edgar Schein of the Sloan School of Management at MIT as "the sum total of all the shared, taken-for-granted assumptions that a group has learned throughout its history." According to Schein, some of the levels of culture include artifacts (the visible organizational structures and processes), espoused values (strategies, goals, and philosophies), and underlying assumptions (unconscious, taken-for-granted beliefs and perceptions). These levels of culture were all present at ToolCo.

It became apparent during the interviews with ToolCo personnel that several dynamics were at play in the organization. These included a widespread variance in understanding of the overall direction of the organization.

"Specifically, where we are going I do not know. I know we are trying to open new markets."

"Some talk about getting into some more international markets that we are not getting. Not outlined as well as it should be."

"Yes, they do have some type of long-range strategic plan, but I do not know the specifics of it."

"Some of the employees understand the vision, some do not. They do not because, I think, the notion of changing the organization to achieve that vision just doesn't fit with their notion of how you manage a business."

"I think they have a picture of what they hope is going to happen."

This variance manifested itself in a continuum range, with a disparity in shared vision at one end of the continuum, to no clear understanding of the vision at the other. Without a clearly understood shared vision of the future, it makes sense that the people in the organization seem lost and disconnected.

Another dynamic that was quite apparent was that the level of communication was largely perceived to be inconsistent, authoritative, and myopically focussed. This was evidenced by the implicit beliefs about one of the types of meetings that were held at ToolCo. Monthly update meetings were designed to communicate important information to a management group. It was apparent from the employee interviews that the meetings were thought of as a one-way communications vehicle – a convenient way to "tell" but not to "learn" about the organizational direction and the issues facing the organization.

"When I first started with the company, I appreciated the update meetings from the standpoint that it is letting everybody know where we stand. I am finding out, more than not, I am the only one sitting in the meetings presenting anything – the finances. I could do that by putting a piece of paper up on the board. And at this point, I don't see the value (in the meetings)."

"I don't believe that you will get an open conversation among peers in a large room like that with some of the managers there. There are some managers who are not real open to criticism."

"Monthly update meetings, do people ask questions? Yes. Do they ask tough questions? Not as tough as they could be. Why is that? Because they don't get the answers or because it isn't safe to ask questions? I think that there is probably some fear involved. Within the management group there are some managers who are more open to those types of questions or dialogs than other managers. At those update meetings usually all the top management group is there. I think there is an intimidation outlook there."

With a dynamic that implicitly prevents employees from raising substantive issues – issues they feel they need to resolve – employees will not feel comfortable resolving questions that impact their ability to be personally effective and, therefore, help the organization become as effective as possible.

The issue of competitive threat facing the ToolCo organization surfaced in every interview. Although there was a relatively high understanding of the threat from other countries due to the fluctuations in currency valuations, there seemed to be little comprehension of what could be done about it. This mismatch between what was understood and what could be understood is a reflection of the apparent organizational belief in single-loop learning as a way to support business.

In single-loop learning (Argyris and Schon, 1992) people understand problems on an individual level. That is to say that the problem at hand is a stand-alone problem and can be 'fixed' through an intervention. Unfortunately, as Fig 1.1 shows, the model identifies the mismatch between outcomes and expected outcomes. This mismatch results in an intervention on the strategic level, i.e. the way the problem is attacked.

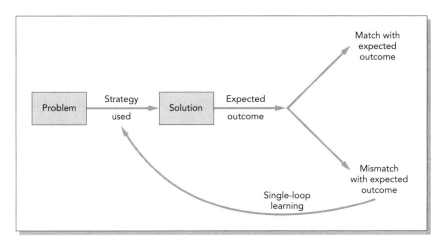

Fig 1.1 How single-loop learning works

Single-loop learning is better than no learning at all, but it does reinforce the belief that by simply changing strategies to reduce the impact of the problems, effective solutions can sometimes be obtained. In the case of ToolCo, it was apparent that the word "effective" referred to solutions that would remain and work over time. However, ToolCo and other companies have come to learn that single-loop learning is not enough in today's world as the solutions that they have counted on have not proved to remain and work over time.

Argyris and Schon's work on learning identifies another learning model, double-loop learning, in which it is possible to look at how we understand a problem-solving process. Double-loop learning takes place when it is recognized that the solution utilized does not result in the expected outcome. This mismatch, instead of causing the development of a new intervention, causes a shift in the mental models that contributed to an understanding of the problem and the strategy determined to resolve it (*see* Fig 1.2).

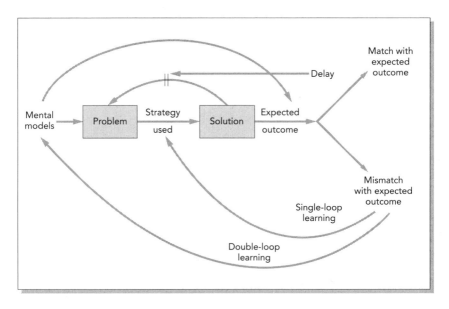

Fig 1.2 The double-loop learning model

As mental models are influenced by the mismatch between outcomes and expected outcomes, our mental models of what the outcomes might be are influenced as well. In addition, it is possible to recognize that solutions may impact the problem itself after a delay. According to Daniel Kim, "problems do not exist independently of the person who sees them." This statement, and its relationship to the concept of double-loop learning, was impacting the ToolCo employee's ability to resolve some of the problems the company was facing.

"If this division is going to survive it either has to buy another company that has a competitive product that we can market, and there has been talk of that, or we have to start to develop a product that we can market that will carry this company into the next 100 years."

This statement is a classic example of single-loop learning. To stay competitive, the apparent options are either to engage in another merger – a strategic remedy that has been used in the past – or to develop a competitive product. The interviews produced no statements that identified the interrelationship between the collective organizational perceptions of the problem and the problem itself.

The almost obvious problem responses for ToolCo (become more flexible, streamline, etc. – all single-loop learning) were evident, but what was missing were the ramifications of those actions or an understanding of how those actions would create lasting change – double-loop learning. This gap in understanding stems from one of several conditions:

- the belief that one cannot provide input;
- the belief that one is not supposed to know;
- apathy, i.e. "it is not my job," or "someone else will take care of the problem."

Without a clear understanding about the organizational strategies to deal with competition, the potential to deal with it *effectively* will be diminished greatly.

Many of the issues that surfaced during the interviews with ToolCo personnel illuminated the culture of the company. Through the interview process, it became clear that there was a feeling in the organization that the two distinct population groups – engineering and administration – would never see the same picture. It is this dynamic, one of opposing views, that can begin to stimulate and reinforce the belief in the "rightness" of each viewpoint. It is this feeling of rightness that has closed the door to a shared vision for the future of the organization, and continues to do so. Additionally, it is the perceived rightness of beliefs that is mitigating the organizational potential to deal effectively with the interrelated issues of communications and competition.

In order for the organization to get past this point, it was imperative to begin a dialog to bring into the open all the issues that were floating below the level of organizational visibility but could not be discussed. To accomplish this, it was necessary to establish an environment where it was "safe" to talk about the issues, one in which dialog was the vehicle that could create it.

Dialog is a word that roughly translates from two Greek words – dia (meaning "through" or "with each other") and logos (meaning "the word"). The most commonly understood definition of the word dialog is "a sustained collective inquiry into everyday experience and what we take for granted" (Issacs, 1993).

The ToolCo organization's technology solution to improve its capacity had taken on a life of its own. Tied directly to the organizational cultural dynamics, the beliefs associated with the technology system and its implementation were something that the organization had to deal with in the immediate future. Whenever an organization implements a technology-based solution to effectiveness, capacity, and communications, it also needs to explore the dynamics of the implementation itself. In the case of ToolCo, as with so many other organizations moving in the same direction, the issue of changing the utilization of technology was not an issue of "will we do it?" but one of "how will we deal with this change?" This, too, is interrelated with the beliefs of the two groups of people in the company and their perceived beliefs about how they see their worlds and the world around them.

How to increase organizational alignment

First, we need to remember that organizational alignment is nothing more than a large number of employees in a company all "seeing" the same picture. This picture can be where the organization is going (its collective vision), what its goals are (what it is trying to accomplish), its values (the way the employees treat each other and customers), and climate (the way people feel about working in the company), to mention a few.

> ● We need to remember that organizational alignment is nothing more than a large number of employees in a company all "seeing" the same picture.

The apparent lack of alignment in the ToolCo organization about how to resolve many of the fundamentally systemic problems they were facing is symptomatic of many organizations. Organizational alignment is a term that has been bantered about for several years. In most cases, it refers to the level of "same sightedness" of a group of people in a company in how they perceive where the organization is going, what their collective purpose is, and how they will achieve the goals and objectives of the organization. Alignment has a relationship to the potential effectiveness of an organization, both currently and in the future. Although there has been much written about the need for alignment in organizations, there has been little discussion on how to increase the level of alignment. There are several reasons for this. These include the fact that organizational alignment is largely thought of as an intangible – alignment is a perception, and on any given day it may shift due to both internal and external factors. In the case of ToolCo, alignment, or the lack of it, was a clear mitigating factor in the organization's inability to move past its current environmental situation and into one in which it could increase its potential to become more viable over time.

To ensure the highest potential for organizational effectiveness, it is important that the majority of the people in a company have the same basic understanding of the organizational mission, vision, and goals – in short, what is important to the organization. Without a common understanding, the potential for organizational success and, therefore, high levels of effectiveness will be diminished. The key words here are "majority" and "common understanding."

Alignment does not mean all the employees in a company marching in single-file formation over the hill together. This type of alignment requires no thought, no understanding. It simply means that each person needs only to do what the person in front of them does. This can lead to disasters – if the person in front stumbles and falls, the ones behind will do the same. Nor does it mean that all the employees in a company are lined up next to one another marching forward. This too can lead to disasters – employees are able to "see" only the people next to them, and are not able to "see" the big picture. Organizational alignment does mean that the vast majority of a population sees the same basic picture, understands that picture, and is moving forward collectively. No lock-step marching, no moving forward without understanding, no lemming-like drives toward a precipice. Alignment is generated by having things in the same perspective for employees to see – the vision, the mission, and the goals and objectives. By increasing organizational alignment in a thoughtful way, it is possible to gain high-leverage benefits for the organization as a whole (*see* Fig 1.3) – organizational effectiveness, reduction in perceived complexity, increases in flexibility, and dilution of potential organizational defense mechanisms.

Organizational effectiveness over time	A more effective organization can meet more customers' needs and, therefore, become more profitable
Reduction in complexity	Complexity is partially due to the lack of common understanding of processes and procedures
Flexibility	To become more flexible and adaptable to new situations requires high alignment in both the need and the methods to achieve flexibility
Dilution of organizational defenses	Defense mechanisms are mitigated and diluted by high visibility and understanding of both the why and the how an organization is changing

Fig 1.3 Alignment benefits rationale

As organizational alignment increases, other behaviors that impact the effectiveness potential change. With more alignment, the ability to increase organizational capacity increases, there is a higher potential for team and collective learning, and there is less variance in the mental models that can severely hinder organizational potential.

In order to increase alignment in a company, it is first necessary to determine the current alignment level. Perhaps the best way to do this is simply to ask the employees. This is not to suggest sending out a survey asking what people think the mission, vision, and goals are – that traditionally results in high percentages of common responses, but common responses to a survey determine nothing more than the ability to remember what they have been told or have overheard. Additionally, getting common responses to traditional surveys will have a tendency to identify perceptions and beliefs that are espoused, but not necessarily beliefs that are manifested in actions.

Espoused beliefs are good to know, but alignment can and does shift when the "rubber hits the road." Organizations are collections of human beings, and one of the driving influences on collective organizational actions is human behaviors. When humans find themselves in situations that they do not necessarily expect or are not prepared for, they tend to figure behaviors that are not congruent with their espoused beliefs. This disconnection comes from an inability or perceived inability to logically determine the relationship between stimulus (the impact of actions on our beliefs) and response (our actions) (Covey, 1989). Therefore, being able to identify beliefs that will drive action is far more critical to the long-term success of an organization. To obtain a more effective measurement of organizational alignment requires digging past surface responses to the meanings behind how a group of employees will act.

Determining the current environment – the survey method

In the October 1995 issue of *The Systems Thinker*, Greg Zlevor wrote an article about community in organizations. The article identified a "community continuum," a theoretical line that showed the various levels of organizational community. The stages that Zlevor identified included disciety (a conjunction of dysfunctional and society), dysfunctional, functional, formative, and community. According to Zlevor, each of these stages or places on the continuum can be identified by the statements that people make about their organization (*see* Fig 1.4). The identifiers of each stage of community have been used quite successfully to help measure the level of alignment within companies. This has been done through the use of a simple survey. It is important to note here that the survey is not used to tell whether there is alignment directly but to determine why the level of alignment in an organization is what it is.

Disciety	This is war. Every person for him or herself.
Dysfunctional	This place is so political. I see glimpses of kindness, but usually feel beat up. I protect myself.
Functional	I do my part, they do theirs. As long as I keep to myself and do my job, I'm ok.
Formative	People cooperate. We have our ups and downs, but mostly ups. There's a fair amount of trust. I can usually say what is on my mind.
Community	I can be myself. I feel safe. Everyone is important. Our differences make us better. We bring out the best in each other.

Fig 1.4 The stages of organizational community

Please respond by placing a check mark after the description that most appropriately identifies how you perceive the current working environment in our organization.

1   This is war. Every person for him or herself.

2   This place is so political. I see glimpses of kindness, but usually feel beat up. I protect myself.

3   I do my part, they do theirs. As long as I keep to myself and do my job, I'm ok.

4   People cooperate. We have our ups and downs, but mostly ups. There's a fair amount of trust. I can usually say what is on my mind.

5   I can be myself. I feel safe. Everyone is important. Our differences make us better. We bring out the best in each other.

All survey responses will be confidential and data will only be published in the aggregate form.

Fig 1.5 Organizational working environment survey

A sample of how this survey vehicle can be used can be found in Fig 1.5. Although quite simple in design, before using it, it is important to consider several things. First, it is helpful when sending out this type of survey to ensure that the respondents cannot be identified in any way, thus guaranteeing more openness in the responses. If someone is being asked to describe an organizational environment, he or she might be hesitant to reply openly if they feel that their response could be tracked to them. Once, when I used this format, several recipients rang my office to inquire as to the need for "honesty" in their response. I was amazed at the question. Upon telling the callers that, yes, I was looking for honesty in a response, I was told, "then why did you put my name on the form?" I immediately checked and found out that the organization's internal mailing system was one in which, to send out any type of internal mail, all you needed to do was put a recipient's name on the item. The surveys had been prepared by an internal resource with the instructions to mail them to the internal management team. At the time, I had no idea of the internal mailing system. **Always know the system you use when asking for responses to potentially sensitive questions!**

Second, simplicity in a request is a key to a high response level. If a survey form is complex, it may dissuade people from responding – too much effort required may equate to reduction in the response level. **Simplify, simplify, simplify!**

Third, it is helpful if the information obtained from the surveys is made visible to the organization upon completion. Withholding information that relates to an organizational environment tends to send the signal that the environment is worse than anyone thought, and it is even too terrible to raise in public. The entire purpose of gathering the information is to be able to begin a conversation about what the information says, both directly and indirectly. **Always make survey results visible!**

Fourth, the responses should only be published in an aggregate form. This is common sense. If the issue is 'organizational' alignment, the results should speak to the organization population as a whole, not to the individuals that comprise it. **Be aware of the population you are asking questions of and, later, sharing the information with!**

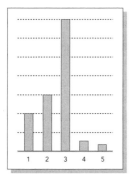

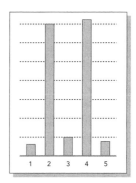

Fig 1.6
An organization with a moderate level of alignment

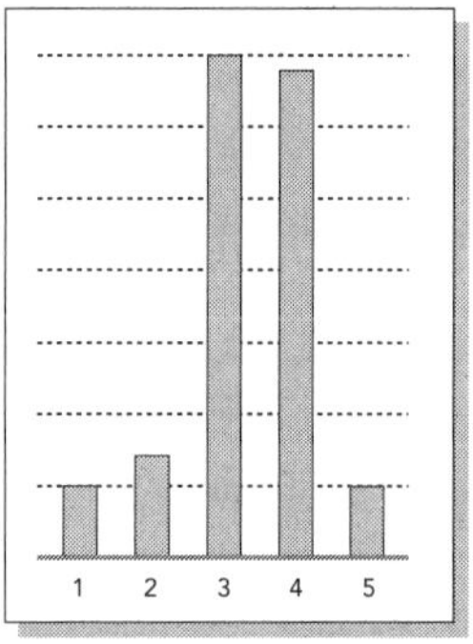

Fig 1.7
A high level of alignment in thinking

Fig 1.8
An organization with no alignment in thinking

Once the surveys have been collected – in some cases by a third party – the responses are totaled and displayed in a histogram format. The level of organizational alignment relating to the questions is quite visible. An organization that has a high level of alignment will have a distribution pattern that is concentrated in one area – a more even distribution would lead one to the conclusion that there is less alignment. Examples of survey responses give other messages as well. Figure 1.6 shows an organization that has a moderate level of alignment. Although the responses are not especially high in the columns on the right side of the graph (columns 4 and 5), the issue here is not what the responses were but the level of alignment in the collective responses. Figure 1.7 shows a high level of alignment in thinking. Although the alignment spans two columns (columns 3 and 4), the fact that these two columns represent the vast majority of thinking in the responses tells a significant story. Figure 1.8, however, represents an environment that is problematic – little alignment in thinking and a high level of apparent chaos in their culture. This example begs several questions. "How can some people see the organization in such a different light?" (note the difference between the statements that comprise the survey, statements 2 and 4). "How can an organization survive when the respondents may feel that on one day, statement 2 is the most appropriate, and on another day, statement 4 is most appropriate?" "What type of environment would generate an almost perfectly bi-modal, symmetrical graph output?" I have seen responses like each of the examples, and in the case of Fig 1.8, have asked all three questions, of myself and of members of the company I am working with. Whatever the answers are, it is critical to realize that the answers that I was given merely generated more questions, for the answers represented only the tip of the iceberg of why an organization acts in the way it does.

Things to remember

When using a survey like the one in Fig 1.5, what to look for is the concentration of responses – it is this that sheds light on the level of alignment. Given a choice between an acceptable response pattern and a realistic look at the level of alignment, I will always look for the level of alignment.

> ● Alignment in the belief that an organization is a terrible place to work can be the signal that there is room for improvement.

Alignment in the belief that an organization is a terrible place to work can be the signal that there is room for improvement. Lack of alignment only leads to reduced effectiveness over time, thereby having the tendency to potentially defeat any improvement efforts.

It is also important to realize that alignment, as seen in survey results, does not imply that the collective actions of a group of employees will necessarily be congruent with the stated goals of the organization. But it should be recognized that without alignment, collective efforts will be fragmented, resulting in diminished performance capacity over time.

Determining the current environment
– the inquiry method

The inquiry method of determining organizational alignment is, on the surface, quite simple – just verbally ask the subject population a set of questions. The issue then becomes, "what questions can we use?" My experiences in this area have shown me that trying to determine alignment requires insights as to how a population perceives the organization from the perspectives of where the organization is and where it is believed to be going. Asking these questions directly can produce "hoped for" responses and, consequently, is of little value. A more effective set of questions that still yields the necessary information would be questions that enable the respondents to think in terms of analogy. This gives the population the ability to respond more accurately to how they perceive the organization without feeling constrained by the feeling of speaking directly for or against the organization or its management. Joe Coletti, a friend and associate, gave me a variation of analogy questions relating to forms of transportation, most often centered on an automobile. The use of transportation as a metaphor for the organization is easy for the employee to connect to, i.e. the organization is seen as something that is moving. It has a condition that either enables or reduces its ability to make that movement, and it is visible. By using the automobile as the focus of the analogy, the respondents can make a strong connection to the organization as a whole.

Analogy questions

Through the utilization of a facilitator, each of these questions can be posed to a collection of potential respondents (*see* Fig 1.9). In question 1, the elements to look for are the specifics of the type of car, its age and perhaps even its color. By using this inquiry method, I have learned that:

- newer cars can be perceived to be associated more closely with technology and its application within an organization;
- more expensive cars can be associated with value and a desire to own;
- bright, flashy colors can be associated with excitement about the organization;
- sportier cars can be associated with organizational responsiveness and agility;
- newer utility vehicles can be associated with organizational ruggedness and ability to survive "rough" organizational times.

These associations are not meant to be absolute in their perceived meanings, only a way to help sort out some of the perceptions of those who have responded to the questions over time.

1	If your organization was some type of vehicle, what kind of vehicle would it be?
2	What condition is this vehicle in today? Be as descriptive as possible.
3	What part of the vehicle are you? (You cannot be a driver or passenger, you must be a component part of the vehicle.)
4	What kind of vehicle do you believe the organization will be next year?

Fig 1.9 Car questions

In question 2, the specifics to look for include the overall automobile condition. Does it have dents? Is there rust on it? Has it been maintained at regular recommended intervals? Most of these questions target how the investment in the car (organization) is taken care of. Is there a concern for the long-term potential of the car (organization)? Does the concern lead to re-investment in the car (organization) through suggested service (training), washing (keeping the organization visible), and providing necessary repairs (keeping current with technology)?

Question 3 is not looking for alignment-related issues but for perceptions of personal value to an organization. The respondents should be instructed that they cannot identify themselves as either the driver or the passenger in an automobile, but must be an actual component of the car. By asking what part of the car the respondent is, the intent is to identify whether the respondent feels that he or she is contributing to the organization and its success. Does the person feel that he or she is the headlights – creating the visibility of leadership? Is the person a wheel – a facilitator helping the organization move forward? Is the person the engine – providing the power to move the organization forward? Is the person the fuel – ensuring the organization can continue on its journey?

Question 4 deals with the respondent's belief in the future of the organization. Responses that speak of little or no change in the condition of the car in the future may lead one to believe that there is a disconnection between the stated and the shared vision. A high variance between current and future condition may allude to high goals that may not be obtainable in the view of the respondent.

Once, while using the automobile analogy as a way of better understanding the dynamics of an organization, a senior manager responded that she felt that the organization was "an old yellow school bus, sort of like the one on *The Partridge Family* television show of the 1970s. You know, all battered, covered with multi-color paint and decals. It has a large luggage rack on the roof and is dragging a large, rusted and dented trailer." She said that she was a seat in the back of the bus, and that the next year's vehicle would be the same, but with a larger trailer. When I heard this, I asked why she said what she did – the prerogative of a facilitator, and in this case especially, I was quite intrigued. It became clear that the respondent felt that her department was the "dumping ground" for initiatives that were driven by legislation – whether the initiatives were appropriate or not, the organization had to do them, and they were "dumped" on her. This accounted for the size and type of vehicle, as well as her response about being a seat in the bus – a place that people just sit on. The response about the vehicle next year told me that she expected nothing more in the future but the same.

Another time in this organization I used the format of *any* type of vehicle. I was told that the organization was currently an old bi-plane, "you know, like the Wright brothers' plane." When I inquired as to next year's vehicle, I was told, "a space shuttle, you know, like the Challenger." I responded, "isn't the Challenger the shuttle that exploded?" The respondent simply smiled and said yes. It was quite clear that the respondent was in an environment in which he believed that the organization today was quite behind in the way it conducted business, in its systems, and in its ability to survive. And in order to "catch up," it would have to make such a dramatic leap into the future that he thought it would destroy itself. A scary thought, to be in that type of organization. (Note: I later found out that the company did go out of business.)

The responses to these types of questions can be very powerful. **It is up to the facilitator to use inquiry to begin to surface what is behind the metaphors that the respondents use to describe their organization.**

Once the facilitator has queried all the subjects in a given facilitation, the responses can be either kept on the flip charts or plotted in a matrix format. If the objective of the exercise is to illuminate any potential gaps in alignment, this step can be quite important, and can yield substantial information about the gap, and where to put efforts to close it.

The matrix chart that is used shows a relative comparison to questions 1, 2 and 4 in a line format (*see* Figs 1.10–1.13). The two axes of the matrix can be correlated to two distinct alignment issues: the range of respondents' expectations, from low to high, is found in the X-axis; the correlation to organizational reality and future potential is found in the Y-axis. The information on the two axes can be plotted as follows.

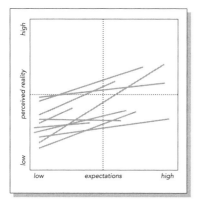

Fig 1.10
High alignment, high potential

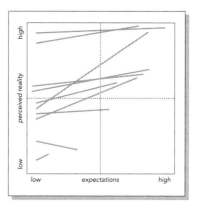

Fig 1.11
High alignment, low potential

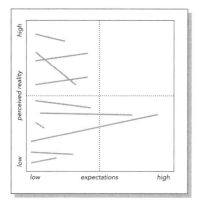

Fig 1.12
Low alignment, low potential

Fig 1.13
Typical alignment, typical potential

If a respondent believes that the organization is not very current, competitive, or technologically state of the art, he or she might have responded to question 1 with an analogy to a vehicle that represents this thought process, i.e. an older model car in less than ideal condition. If his or her perception is that the future potential of the car (next year's automobile model) was good, the vehicle they used in the analogy might resemble a current model or next year's model with all the available accessories. These elements would result in a line that would extend from the lower left-hand corner to the upper right-hand corner. An older car in less than ideal condition with no basic change in the subsequent year would result in a line that was relatively short and parallel to the axis frame. It is important to note that when plotting the responses, the ranges used, i.e. years and conditions of current and future models, are dependent on the collective responses, not on an absolute or fixed basis. This means that the matrix borders should not reflect any specific years, only the high and low ranges of the responses.

An appropriate question at this point might be, so what does a fully charted matrix mean? The responses shown in Fig 1.10 would lead one to believe that this represents a population in which there is a good level of alignment in both the current reality and future potential vision. Figure 1.11 shows a population that has a high level of alignment in the current reality, but little perspective on the potential future vision of the organization. The population group shown in Fig 1.12 appears to be quite scattered, i.e. with very little common understanding of where the organization is and where it is going. The responses plotted in Fig 1.13 are typical – although on the surface they appear to show little alignment, they are actually representative of most organizations.

Most organizations consist of people who have different perspectives – this is the richness of diverse opinions. In the example of Fig 1.13, the population appears to consist of some people with low perceptions of reality and low expectations; some with high perceptions of reality and high expectations; and some in the middle – a centered belief in where the organization is today, and a good expectation that the organization can become something better. This is representative of a matrix that is sought after in today's world – a good level of alignment and a solid grounding in the current reality. **None of the examples shown in Figs 1.10, 1.11, 1.12, and 1.13 is any better or worse than the others. They are all simply graphic representations of the level of alignment in the subject organizations.**

When using a method to try to better understand the level of alignment in an organization, it is important to remember not to get "lost" in the data. The data collected is used only as a vehicle to both enhance the understanding of the level of alignment and to create a place to begin to have a conversation about that level. The chart is that vehicle and should not be considered to be the "answer" – the chart is the impetus to begin the questions about why an organization is where it is and why it is there.

Organizational alignment is important. However, the level of alignment does not preclude individuality in thinking, diversity in opinions, or varying perspectives. Alignment does not mean that everyone needs to follow in lock-step with senior management and their decisions. But without high levels of alignment – a collective clear understanding of where an organization is, where it is going, how it will get there, and why it is moving in that direction – the potential of an organization will never be achieved. Alignment is a way to help an organization realize its potential.

Summary

It is like driving at night, through the woods, in the fog, on a winding road, with no headlights

How we will be able to ensure our company's success

ToolCo is a company that has existed for a long time because it knew what it was doing, and knew how to do it well. But the times have changed, and ToolCo may have been left behind. In order to "catch up," ToolCo's management decided that it needed to put forward several initiatives that would make it competitive once again. But in the process of doing this, the management encountered what it believed were complex dynamics. What it believed to be complex was in fact quite simple – there was too little alignment among the employees of ToolCo about where they were going, why they were going in that direction, and how they would get there. The efforts of management began to shift from making decisions about how to best move toward their future to activities that focussed on simply holding the company together. This was a deep spiral – a spiral that would cause the company to lose sight of its vision and its ability to be sustainable over time. By focussing on building alignment in the organization, management's efforts could once again focus on what was important and creative, not on matters that were urgent and reactive.

Key learning

It is critical to always ensure that the employees of an organization clearly understand where an organization is going, why it is going there, and what the benefits of heading in that direction are. Without this clarity, the employees will lose sight of what is important to help the organization, and consequently the potential of the organization may never be achieved.

2

Gee, I thought the draft ended years ago

How to avoid a "forced march" mentality on project teams

When organizations undergo dynamic changes in the way they operate, it is crucial to make the employees of a company aware of how they fit into the new structure. In many cases, this problem is dealt with by increasing the level of involvement on the part of the population. In today's world, this makes sense.

During the 1900s a shift from the belief that workers are employed to do what they are told, a belief pattern that was in place earlier in the century, when Frederick Taylor and Henry Ford set the tone for the relationship between management and workers. In the past decade, we have seen this thinking shift more toward the belief that the employees of an organization just may have insights as to a better way to run an organization, better ways to be an effective organization. This shift in thinking has resulted in higher levels of involvement in the short and long-term planning processes of organizations. In many cases, this could be deemed to be good. But in some organizations, the way in which this is accomplished can result in more damage than the good it can do.

The story of ConnectCo is one such story. ConnectCo is a typical company in today's world, an organization that is a result of an acquisition strategy over the past half-decade. The senior management of ConnectCo determined that to ensure that all the acquisitions could be effectively acculturated into the newly evolving structure, it would put together a team of representatives from each of the three largest business units. The purpose of this team was to help determine how best to figure out how to have an organization with one culture – a task that would be difficult in an organization that had made 12 acquisitions in five years. On the surface, this strategy appears to be sound. But by reading the story, we soon find that it is rarely "what" an organization does that is wrong; it is "how" the organization does it that causes trouble.

ConnectCo

ConnectCo is a relatively young computer technology accessory company. The company has shown extraordinary growth in the past five years, much of it achieved through an implicit strategy of acquisition. At the time of researching material for this book, ConnectCo had just completed its latest acquisition, of a company in the same field as itself but with a different product mix. In the process of researching how the employees of ConnectCo were dealing with all the changes it had experienced, I interviewed members of a cross-functional work team that had been assembled to integrate the various disparate population groups that had been acquired into one effective organizational structure.

This team, which I will call the XF (for "cross-functional") Team, consisted of members of business units from three distinct sites, each in different geographic locations throughout the United States. Additionally, the team had as advisers and facilitators two consultants from an external organization. Their purpose was to help guide the team through improving processes and effectiveness for the firm overall.

Initial interviews with the team began to show several things. First, it became apparent that the external consultants had more information about the team and its purpose than did the team members. Second, the team members were all operating from different levels of information, and third, the team members had many concerns about what their real charge was. These items began to surface both during the interview process and through observations of team meetings.

It became clear that many of the team members were unsure of how they were assigned to participate in the team, and were concerned about their ability to continue to be effective in their day-to-day jobs of responding to customers, due to the number and duration of team meetings. As the team began to meet, some team members expressed concerns and confusion about the purpose of the team and how they would make decisions. In an effort to move these concerns into the open, the consultants spent quite a bit of time facilitating training in what they said were traditionally considered "soft skills" – core competencies of vision, understanding, and systemic thinking. This began to raise additional concerns on the part of team members, as they believed that they should be focussing their time on ways to improve the overall effectiveness of the team and, consequently, the organization. Many of the team believed that this facilitation process was not a productive use of their time.

"The XF Team was initially put together without an explicit purpose, and then the team sort of defined the purpose."

"We need to better define our objectives, how we are going to meet them, and what the criteria is for meeting them. When some objectives were picked, we didn't know how to measure them."

"One of our objectives is something like two sentences long and completely general, like, 'we're going to train our employees and we are going to make sure that everybody has what they need to succeed.' If the objective is to have everybody succeed, then we should say what he or she needs to succeed. Doing it this way may not go over well with all regions. We have done stuff differently for a long time and this may be more difficult to change for some than others."

These comments illustrated the belief among the team that their work was new and untested in their environment. Dealing with changes like this in an organization can cause uneasiness on the part of all employees, not just the ones directly being impacted by the change process. And this uneasiness was magnified by the team members as they were the group charged with developing the change process.

The XF Team experiment appeared to be a success at the time of the interviews. They had been meeting for about 12 months, and had grown quite a bit. What was interesting was the approach that was taken by the team and facilitators to deal with the problems and issues as they surfaced. Most visible of the problems and issues was how the team could attain alignment in their growth process, why they were together, and what management's expectations were for their future – all as a result of the implicit growth structure of the organization.

"Sometimes we seem to have a lack of focus which causes lots of frustration, but when push comes to shove, we kind of step up to the plate and we all kind of pull each other along."

"When we were first put on the team we felt that what we were doing was kind of crazy and it was pulling us away from our work where we had so much to do."

These perceptions can lead one to assume that some of the team members did not comprehend that learning what was important was the same as work. In my experience, this connection of "traditional" work with work, and learning with non-value added time, is pervasive in most organizations, especially in those that have a historical pattern of being a "fast-moving" organization. I have seen this in many organizations that espouse the value of learning, but as soon as the "numbers" that drive the business begin to fall, learning falls by the wayside as it is not as important as the "work."

The XF Team had been traveling on a journey that had seen some successes and some ongoing and recurring problems. The team identified these in the interview process. Their successes included:

● team learning – the team were able to learn both individually and collectively;

● community building – the team were able to "connect" with each other, building trust in each other's actions;

● realization of the importance of cultural values – the team were able to identify the values which they operated under, and were willing to hold these values in high regard as a way to meet and work together;

● unplanned measurable outcomes – the team were able to identify and recommend process changes that were measurable and of value to the overall organization.

Some of the issues and problems included:

● the need for clarity in the management and team vision – the team wanted to increase the ability of themselves and others in the organization to "see" where they and the organization were going;

● a "hazy" purpose definition with measurable outcomes – the team wanted management to make their purpose more explicit and specifically identify expected outcomes from the team's efforts;

- how to communicate outcomes throughout the organization – the team struggled with how to ensure that the organization would be able to clearly understand what the team was doing, and what the team had accomplished;

- how to synergize with different personalities and types – the team, being comprised of various members from multiple sites and with different personality and learning styles, struggled with how to improve their capacity to work together, and to shorten the learning curve of this process;

- how to relax the tension over trust and "safety" – as the team went through the various stages of development, they experienced concerns about their ability to trust each other and create an environment that was safe enough to let trust occur.

> In most organizations, the level of tolerance for dealing with the delay between team formation and expected team results is quite small.

In most organizations, the level of tolerance for dealing with the delay between team formation and expected team results is quite small. This can be due to many things, the most visible of which is the real and/or perceived pressure from stakeholders. In the case of the XF Team, however, the level of tolerance appeared to be quite high. This could have been the apparent lack of organizational-wide knowledge on the activities of the team. Regardless of the reason, the level of tolerance relating to team formation and team results can be a key contributor to the potential for long-term success.

This dynamic can be seen in Fig 2.1. This figure represents the interrelationships of variables that can impact organizational learning. As learning increases, it contributes to organizational understanding, and this leads to a higher tolerance of ambiguity, cultural differences, and multiple perspectives. As this tolerance increases, the potential for long-term success increases, resulting in additional organizational learning. This structure does not imply that teams cannot learn from the lack of success. In reality, people and teams of people can and do learn from "failures." But as the structure shows, although learning can take place regardless of success or the lack of it, learning itself is interrelated to understanding and a tolerance for ambiguity – this is the opposite of "fixed" beliefs that are not open to change, i.e. learning. The dynamics shown in the structure are reinforcing in nature – all the variables change in the same direction. This is both good

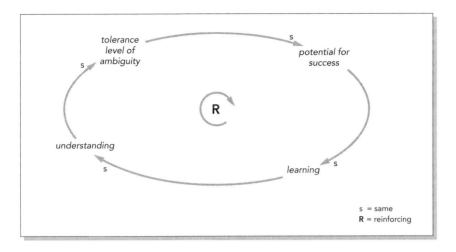

Fig 2.1 The interrelationships of variables that can impact organizational learning

news and bad news. The good news is that as learning increases, understanding increases. The bad news is that as learning decreases, understanding decreases. The lesson here is to explore what the ConnectCo XF Team was facing: "How could the team continue to learn?"

"I think the team is doing the right stuff and I have seen changes already. I feel that it has been a little painful at times, but some people don't like what we are doing by forcing decision making down on them and really making them think about the issues and not falling back on their managers to make every decision."

For an organization to learn to become more effective, it must recognize that learning is everyone's responsibility. This has a strong connection to the need for double-loop learning in organizations. By having managers make all the decisions, only single-loop learning is likely to take place, i.e. learning what to do. The understanding and utilization of double-loop learning as a way to conduct business will be the key to long-term organizational success, i.e. learning "why" it is important.

> ● For an organization to learn to become more effective, it must recognize that learning is everyone's responsibility.

Just as in the work with ConnectCo, whenever an organizational team is working on improving organizational effectiveness, there are two things that need to be done:

- **Document the learning process** Through the documentation process, it is possible to determine whether the team actually did learn anything. Additionally, the documentation process would create a "trail" of where the team had gone on its journey and how it was able to get to where it is currently. The documentation process would also provide a path for other, similar teams to follow as the learning process moves throughout a group of company employees. Through the learning and documentation process, the work of teams can develop more open and honest communication paths, a deeper understanding of important issues, a reduction in placing blame, and the provision of new ways to address issues that appear to be complex.

- **Disseminate the documented work throughout senior management** This is important for continued team progress. The reason for this is to help counteract any sense of ambiguity on the part of senior management regarding their understanding of the purpose, goals, and outcomes of the team's efforts. Additionally, the dissemination of the work progress would help gain senior management support for ongoing learning.

These two points surfaced during the interviews with ConnectCo personnel.

"I think management is aware but they see what they want to see basically. This type of process is very new for this organization. I think management is aware, but they see it in the way they want to and I think the jury is still out in terms of if management feels like it was worth the time, the money, and the effort."

"It is good to know that management supports us, at least the management we know and deal with. I am not sure how far the support goes, because I don't know how high up people know what we are doing."

The problems and issues faced by the team at ConnectCo are not unique to them. They are faced by teams in organizations of all types that have experienced similar growth patterns due to mergers and acquisitions (Rieley and Leahy, 1998). The impact of merger activity as a growth strategy can be measured in several ways:

- shifts in cultural norms – evidenced by employee satisfaction data;
- employee productivity – evidenced by productivity levels;
- financial performance – evidenced by financial statements.

It should be noted that each of these measures has an impact on the other ones. By exploring that relationship, we can better understand the overall impact on a company employee group.

Summary

Gee, I thought the draft ended years ago

How to avoid a "forced march" mentality on project teams

ConnectCo was on the "fast track." It had a glowing record of growth, and was seen to be moving forward at a rapid rate. In the competitive world of technology, the growth strategy of acquisition made sense. By buying out some of the competition you increase your market share while at the same time eliminating some of the competition – bigger and stronger, all through the growth strategy. In order to increase the ability of the company to more effectively integrate the acquired company populations, ConnectCo management decided to put together a team for the purpose of focussing on assimilation of previously competitive company cultures. But in the process of doing this, they seemed to forget to let the people on the team know as much as they did about not only why they were a team but what being on the team would mean in terms of responsibilities (both as team members and their "normal" jobs), accountabilities (who the team would be accountable to, and what they would be held accountable for), and learning diffusion (how they would be expected to share their learnings with the company as a whole). These "little" oversights by management reduced the potential benefits of the team to the point that team members lost their sense of excitement and challenge, and the team efforts simply became "another job" in the company.

Key learning

When assembling project teams, always ensure that the team members have a clear understanding of the objectives of the team, the responsibilities the team will face, and the level to which the team will be held accountable for their work. Additionally, ensure that the team will be able to see that their efforts are implemented and valued by the senior management of the company.

3

I change by not changing at all

What happens when we try to avoid change initiatives

This chapter explores the dynamics associated with organizations that are undergoing change initiatives. By change initiatives, I mean something that causes a group of employees to be forced to exhibit behaviors that are different to those they have been exhibiting in the past. Needless to say, this means almost any type of organizational initiative – restructuring, implementation of an enterprise resource planning system, a merger or acquisition, a process improvement design, or even simply the roll-out of a new product line. Of all the things that we undergo in our lives, the only constant is change.

In a conference session several years ago, I heard Peter Senge explain this the most succinctly. To paraphrase Senge, the average life of a human cell is measured in weeks or months. All the cells in a human body are constantly renewing themselves by replacing dying cells with new cells. His point was that, based on this fact, we are not the same people we were only months ago. We are constantly experiencing change, and yet for some reason we seem to be resistant to it. This might be due to the fact that most of the changes we experience, and are not concerned with, are subtle changes, changes that we are not even aware of. But when faced with dramatic change – change that really catches our attention – we seem to resist it in almost any way we can. This is not to say that we do not go along with the change, only that we are not comfortable with it and that, if given the option, would rather not experience it.

Some changes we experience are easier to adapt to than others. One of the ways in which this comes to light is through an exercise with people facing organizational change initiatives. Have a group of people pair up and have each pair stand back to back. Ask each of them to change three things about the way they look, and after a few moments, have them turn to face each other. This usually causes people to look for what has changed on their partner. Sometimes the changes are quite visible, sometimes not as visible. Next, ask them to turn round once again and now change four things about themselves. After a few more moments, ask them to turn to face their partner. By now, the exercise will be yielding some humorous examples of change – shoes are reversed, buttons are unbuttoned, hair partings are shifted to the other side of the head, glasses are removed, and other obvious examples. Now ask them to turn round and change five more things about themselves. By now, frustration will be building. "I can't change anything else," and "this isn't fun any more" are some of the comments that might be heard. That is to be expected, as what the participants are experiencing is not easy by this point. Ask them one more time to turn away from their partner and change six things about themselves.

When conducting this exercise, I have rarely got past this point, for the groups I have done this with have been about to rebel. When going through the de-brief of this exercise, several things stand out. First, the initial changes that the group experiences are not difficult, and in the context of a facilitated session they are almost always considered to be fun. But by the second or third or fourth time, the exercise has ceased to be easy and fun. In fact, most people begin to struggle with their ability to continually change something about themselves. Second, it is relatively easy to make the comparison with the shift from easy to difficult in the exercise with the amount of changes that organizations ask their people to go through when changing the way in which the organization does business. Minor changes in organizational policies and procedures are not too difficult to deal with, but being subjected to what seem to be ongoing, never ending requests to change becomes more and more difficult over time. This, in an organization, leads to resistance to change and examples of how people try to make it appear that changes are happening when in reality they are not. Third, as soon as the exercise is over and the de-brief is going on, the vast majority of the group population begin to "change back" as rapidly as they can. This is another example of our unwillingness to accept the changes that we experience.

Further examples of how we respond to change can be determined through how people respond to three questions. Question 1 is: "How do you feel when you are anticipating a major change in your organization?" Responses typically include:

- nervous
- concerned
- apprehensive
- worried
- frustrated.

Question 2 is: "How do you feel when in the midst of a large organizational change?" Responses include:

- stressed out
- unsure
- lost
- worried.

The last question is: "How do you feel when you have survived a large change initiative implementation?" These answers include:

- better
- relieved
- resigned
- stronger.

All these responses are feelings. They represent an emotional state that people experience when either faced with, surrounded by or having dealt with change. To better understand what is behind these feelings, research has been conducted with employees undergoing change initiatives. These case studies represent people from the manufacturing and service sectors, from healthcare, from education, and from government.

OsirisCo

In November 1996, an investment group purchased a 37-year-old organization I shall call OsirisCo. The organization was suddenly confronted with the prospect of a loss of autonomy and, equally distressing, the loss of its historic identity. In fact, the response to the takeover, however friendly, was immediate and disturbing. After weeks of hushed silence in the halls, concerns were now vocalized about macromanagement, micromanagement, leadership, and individual performance goals. The primary identity questions were pondered: who are we *now*? Where are we going? What should we do and be?

For a time, the buyout felt like a new marriage, with each "partner" acting tentatively, unsure how to act in this new relationship. The parent company sent key personnel to OsirisCo's corporate office to assure the subordinate partner that corporate life would go on, and that existing management would stay in place. (These were "family men," the word circulated, with whom it would be "easy" to work.)

Soon it became apparent that, while corporate life would go on, it would be different. Communication from the parent company began with formal, modestly reassuring announcements and letters. Then it changed, in two ways: first, the level of communications began to decline; second, the content and tone shifted. While OsirisCo's managers anticipated reorgani-zation, it was the sudden termination of four senior executives, including the president and chief operating officer, and the announced closure of 40 percent of the company's offices, that alarmed and behaviorally froze employees.

To try to understand the events of the buyout, and the emotional swings in the organization, a group of employees began to meet to explore the dynamics at work in a corporate takeover. When the group met, they decided to employ the theories, concepts, and tools associated with systems thinking. These tools, they considered, would help them "see" elements of the takeover story that might not be immediately evident. With the guidance of a systems thinking facilitator/consultant, the group began to tell the "story" of OsirisCo before, during, and after the buyout. The group wanted to gain a deeper understanding of the forces that had created in-stability and anxiety in the environment.

While telling a story seemed a simple enough task at first, it proved to be unexpectedly hard work. More than one writer – David Bohm, Peter Senge, William Isaacs, Edgar Schein – has documented the incoherence in our thought and conversation. Besides that, as Senge explains, we have been taught, throughout our time in the education system, not to tell stories, but to answer questions and stick to facts. With some practice of this art, some of the group learned to weave the facts into a story. The group learned to determine a narrative's authenticity, not just by facts but by its rhythm, i.e. by how the parts of the story hung together. Did the story make sense? Was it cohesive? Was the tone off-key? Was it a reflection of the teller's or the community's reality?

The facilitator was faced with a problem common to this type of work. Managers at OsirisCo (and most other companies) are expected to find "fixes" – fast. Slowing down the process, exploring problems, telling and listening to a story, hearing its rhythm, feeling a narrative's authenticity are not part of the typical business curriculum. In other words, managers were asked to engage in "the willing suspension of disbelief for the moment," to unlearn and relearn. The purpose of the group was just to explore the world in which they now lived.

The learning group was aware that different people held different views, even beliefs, about what was happening at OsirisCo. Life experiences and their "mental models" affected their interpretation of the world. As an example, if a member of the group had had a collaborative working relationship with his or her supervisor in the past, the expectation was that future working relationships would be participative. This experience set up different and higher expectations than those of other group members who had had challenging work relationships with their supervisors in the past. As each in the group shared their stories, these perspectives and beliefs became evident. In other words, the past impinged upon the present and the future, even though the venture capitalists and managing directors were not known. The group had to move through the assumptions to the data and the story that lay beneath.

As the members began to relate their narratives, several common themes or variables emerged. Equally important, a common story of the buyout took shape. The group first explored the themes that related to the story (*see* Fig 3.1). The themes they found most compelling and interrelated were charted, thus enabling the group to see how the importance of the themes changed over time.

Figure 3.2 shows the recurring themes in the organization from August 1996 to October 1997. The themes understandably affected each other as they increased or decreased in importance or when they intersected. A theme's resonance in the organization increased or decreased as conditions changed. As communication increased, for instance, fear seemed to decrease; or as the level of understanding of what was occurring and why went down, the "need to survive" went up (*see* Fig 3.1). Seeing this relationship to the conditions at work further sensitized the group: it made

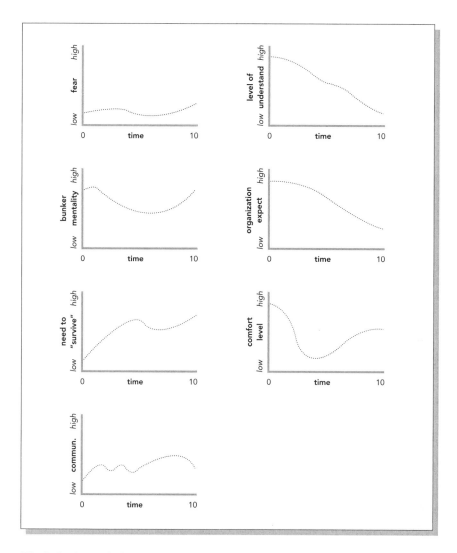

Fig 3.1 Theme behaviors over time

them aware of the fragility of the situation and added to their sense of vulnerability.

Surprisingly, the group continued to dig deeper – surprising because the work became, at times, painful and disconcerting. It pushed toward understanding the main story. The main story seemed to emerge out of the conditions described by the recurring themes that were penetrating the company. Group members recognized after several meetings that central to the story that was unfolding was the company's apparent

Fear	The level of fear that the organization experienced because of an unknown future.
Bunker mentality	The no-risk, "keep-the-head-down" attitude of people trying to ride out the acquisition process.
Need to survive	The organization's feeling about threat of job loss.
Communication	The level of top-down, bottom-up, cross-departmental, open, honest, trusting conversation.
Level of understanding	The recognition of how little managers knew about the short and long-term future of OsirisCo.
Organizational expectations	What the organization held as its collective future participation in the "big picture."
Comfort level	How the organizational population felt about working in the new environment.

Fig 3.2 Themes and definitions at OsirisCo

> ● Group members recognized after several meetings that central to the story that was unfolding was the company's apparent inability to make decisions.

inability to make decisions. It took the group time to consider how this dysfunction potentially affected traditional cultural norms, productivity, and financial performance. Each member individually identified his or her ability/inability to make decisions on a "behavior over time" chart. The results, although showing variation, yielded significant learning (*see* Fig 3.3).

Considered collectively, the charts revealed that in "current" time (September 1997) the group's ability to make decisions was less than at the time of the buyout. Second, the group discovered that, even before the buyout, the ability to make decisions was not especially high (about 6 on a scale of 10). In its traditional, command-and-control pyramid, decisions made at OsirisCo required the approval of management – lots of them. The group was learning what it was like to bump up against changing cultural norms and how that affected management behavior. In the "old" culture, the time and energy to get a decision "made" was exceptional, but group members *knew* the decision makers and knew the *process* for decision making. Neither was known now. As the group's learning progressed,

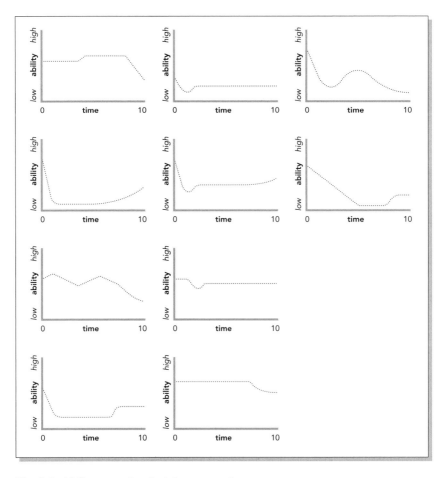

Fig 3.3 Ability to make decisions over time

members began to rely as much on the authenticity of their feelings, percep-tions and stories as they did on the "known" facts of the buyout. This was, however small, a revolution in the making! The group, it is axiomatic, was not making science. Nor was it occupied just with process mapping. The methods were not scientific, nor the tools exclusively from the total quality management (TQM) toolbox. Something else was in use.

The group had strong feelings and were able to hold those feelings and work with them and the actions or dysfunctions they caused. These feelings were related in the form of themes, narrative strands, and stories. The facil-itator then began to structure the stories into a meaningful whole. The facil-itator focussed on several themes and causally linked them in a map. The story, up until now, had been composed of different themes, a series of

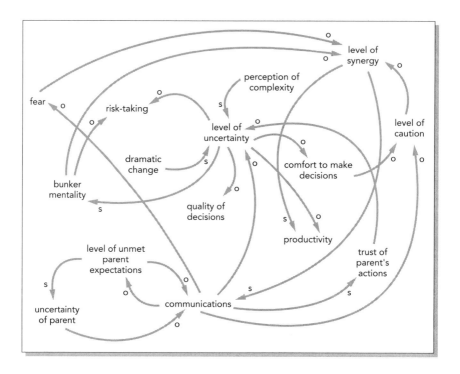

Fig 3.4 Relationships of themes

components. As Peter Senge points out: "The defining characteristic of a system is that it *cannot* be understood as a function of its isolated components. First, the behavior of the system doesn't depend on what each part is doing but on how each part is interacting with the rest ... Second, to understand a system we need to understand how it fits into the larger system of which it is a part."

The themes causally linked to the story of the company's ability to make decisions were the group's "level of uncertainty" and the group's "access to information". The causal map that was developed appeared as a chaotic array of themes and arrows pointing to themes (*see* Fig 3.4). The arrows show the relationship of one theme to another. The letters associated with the arrows identify the direction of the theme as it increases or decreases resonance. An "s" denotes a same-direction impact, i.e. as one theme's resonance increases, the other increases or grows as well. As one decreases, the other also decreases. An "o" denotes an opposite-directional impact, i.e. as one theme's resonance increases, the other decreases. As one decreases, the other increases.

In this "map" or causal web, the relationships begin to become clearer: when the buyout occurred, the level of uncertainty increased, affecting the comfort level with making decisions, which decreased. This condition led to an increase in the organization's level (as represented by the learning group) of caution. Increased caution resulted in decreased levels of synergy. Decreased synergy led to decreased productivity.

It was not surprising that as OsirisCo tried to understand and adjust to its new parent-owner, the level of synergy went down and the level of communication decreased. Diminished communication, in turn, led to more uncertainty, which affected the level of productivity over time. A disturbing element was also introduced as the group followed the plot of the story. The members tried to imagine the effects of their dysfunctional behaviors on the parent, acquiring company and reached some tentative, but compelling, conclusions. As communications decreased, the level of potential unmet parent expectations increased, resulting in a probable increase of the parent's uncertainty, leading to more reduced communications, and so on. This relational dynamic might, the learning group thought, be an appropriate place for intervention. (The group fully recognized that, in the absence of data about the parent, it was making an assumption; the assumption was treated as a hypothesis.)

The group continued to isolate specific themes that were intimately related and, in the process, deepened their understanding of the dynamics at work in the company. At this point, the facilitator brought back two points about the group's work: that the essence of systems thinking is that there is more going on than meets the eye, and that they were not meeting to try to "fix" anything, but to gain a better understanding of what was occurring.

The group selected the themes whose relationships appeared to be having the greatest impact on the organization's ability to become more effective, i.e. make decisions. The themes were accordingly redrawn into separate causal loops and then correlated to each other. The graphic representation of the dynamics of the story was startling. The picture (Fig 3.5) demonstrated that each of these causal relationships was reinforcing (R). This meant that the effects would continue to build (or decrease) over time. The three loops (R1, R2, and R3) were all sending the same message: unless an intervention was identified and acted upon, organizational effectiveness in the form of decision-making ability would continue to diminish over time.

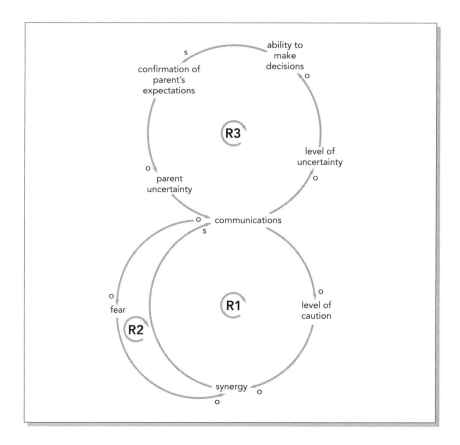

Fig 3.5 Impact of communications

As part of the learning process, the group agreed to explore an intervention that would balance the behavioral relationships. The object of this exploration was to find a potential solution that could reverse the effects of the dynamic at play. An appropriate intervention would improve the company's ability to make a decision. The system's thinking archetype, "Growth and Underinvestment," was discussed to help clarify the dynamics at work.

Systems archetypes are behavioral patterns that appear in organizations of all types. First made clear by a group from MIT more than a decade ago, the archetypes can be used to discover potential interventions that can help managers understand the impact of decisions. The Growth and Underinvestment archetype shows what happens when an organizational growth engine meets a limiting factor and how the impact of the limiting factor can be minimized.

The group began by identifying its growth engine. Class participants chose organizational synergy and the ability to make decisions. Members thought that as the ability of OsirisCo's managers to make decisions increased, the level of synergy in the organization would also increase. Synergy, in turn, would increase the managers' ability to make decisions. This reinforcing behavior (R1) is represented in Fig 3.6.

The limiting factor identified by the group was the lack of clarity in communications and expectations. These recurring themes were developed from the group's previous work. In order to make effective decisions, the group believed that the decision makers at OsirisCo would need to have consistent, honest, two-way communication with the new parent company as well as within their own organization. Additionally, the group believed that to make effective decisions, the OsirisCo managers would need to learn the explicit expectations of the parent.

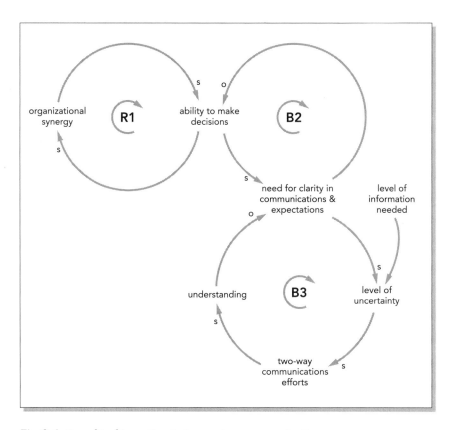

Fig 3.6 Benefit of investing in improving communications

Group expectations included the parent's willingness to share its short and long-term goals, and the parent's desire to relate the short and long-term direction of, and goals for, OsirisCo. The sense that this need was not being met meant the organization's ability to make decisions was being limited, and consequently was limiting its ability to improve productivity over time. This limiting factor makes the dynamics of loop B2 balancing. This balancing behavior would change the positive growth engine (R1) from a virtuous cycle to a vicious cycle, diminishing both the ability of the organization to make decisions and the level of synergy in the organization.

In a Growth and Underinvestment archetype, a second balancing loop is connected to the limiting factor to show the effect on the limit of an intervention. In this case, the group believed that an appropriate intervention was two-way communication. When two-way communication is introduced as a component of the loop, the dynamic changes. As the need for clarity in communication and expectations increases, the level of uncertainty increases – driving the need for increased two-way communication efforts. (The level of uncertainty is determined by an implicit standard on how much uncertainty the organization can "live with" to make effective decisions.) Two-way communication increases understanding and reduces the need for additional clarity. It was the level of two-way communication in place that the group believed was the "underinvestment." If improved, the limiting factor would diminish.

> ● As the need for clarity in communication and expectations increases, the level of uncertainty increases.

While group members had several weeks to ponder this intervention, they also became interested in the consequences to financial performance over time. The finance expert in the group made it clear that the numbers were not pristine. The organization had been acquired as a public company and had been taken private. How numbers were calculated changed somewhat. For example, expenses typically charged to a branch office profit and loss (P&L) were now charged in some cases to "restructuring." However, as a "restructuring" of this magnitude had not been attempted before, OsirisCo's branch managers had never previously had to accept restructuring charges to their P&L. In other words, the numbers over this period were not so far skewed that no comparison could be made.

To try to view the financial dynamic that was unfolding, the group chose to consider revenue and profit. (Revenue and profit seemed the "cleanest" numbers to compare "before and after," and they were the numbers emphasized in an October 1996 letter to OsirisCo employees by the chairman of the parent company.) In its core business, OsirisCo's revenue is made from the contingent fees based on successful completion of its service product. Typically, the revenue stream oscillates, based in part on sales completed in the previous three months. On the profit side, historical pressure on contingency rates put persistent pressure on profits. Expense management was always given high consideration in the OsirisCo of the past. Frequent and intense "paperclip-counting campaigns" – to use Tom Peters' phrase – were not unusual. However, as the group tracked the numbers and paused over the graphs, the "story" of the numbers, as they oscillated across the page, began to take shape.

No one could calculate the precise correlation between financial performance and the story that the group had uncovered. Market conditions had changed; rates for service had changed; internal processes had begun to change; offices had been closed; the workforce, between January and June 1997, had been reduced. However, out of the external and internal conditions, some patterns began to emerge. Between August 1995 and July 1996, the monthly revenue numbers averaged $15.4 million. With the exception of July 1996, which was an aberration, the revenue numbers begin to deteriorate steadily from March. (A one-off sale of assets in July 1996 accounts for the spike in revenue.) About the same time, from February 1996, the contribution or profit before taxes began to soften and then fell to a negative in July (*see* Fig 3.7).

When the group scanned the data points over a 12-month period preceding the sale of the company, the numbers did not invite enthusiasm. Revenue moved down, as did profit. In the past, the company had rung the bell of 20 percent growth, having enjoyed steady revenue improvement between 1976 and 1994. The story that seemed to be at work was a "limits to

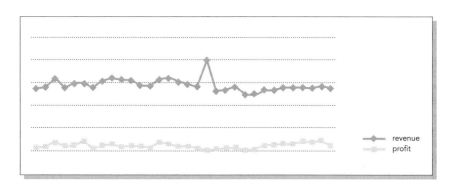

Fig 3.7 OsirisCo's profit before taxes

growth" – the reason, the group concluded, for the sale of the company by OsirisCo's original majority owners. What happened next was the story of the takeover that had been revealed through the group meetings.

By July 1996, rumors of the acquisition became daily conversation. Typical expense-cutting measures (no travel, capital purchases, parties, etc.) were mandated. The company began to shut down. The unspoken – the "undiscussable" – topic was to maintain share price and not go into a negative profit position. The company held on by its fingernails, but the damage had been done. The numbers between August and December 1996 were flat. By the time of the acquisition, the air had gone entirely out of the organizational "balloon." The revenue figure in November 1996 was the lowest in the past 20 months – in fact the lowest number in almost two years. In November, also, the company suffered its largest one-time loss in the past 20 months – in fact it was the greatest monthly loss since late 1993. December proved almost equally distressing: as the company prepared to close more than 12 offices and sack over 400 people, revenue declined further and the company again operated at a loss. Rumors of office closures fueled the anxiety level, particularly at OsirisCo's corporate headquarters. Between July and November 1996, the company was in the state of "getting ready for the sale."

From the new year, however, the numbers improved, compared with November–December. But as profit moved up, revenue trends remained stagnant. Between August 1996 and July 1997, profit grew by more than 36 percent and revenue declined 16 percent compared with the 12 months between August 1995 and July 1996. As offices closed, expense was taken out, even with the gradual rise in headcount to near pre-acquisition levels. Attention had shifted from a public company focus on revenue to a private company focus on cash flow and profit. Consultants focussed on technical and process inefficiencies and unprofitable clients. Managers concentrated on the profitable clients, and marketers began the unpleasant task of shedding unprofitable clients or raising rates. At the time of writing, there were marginal improvements everywhere.

But as people emerged from the bunker, there was – and still is – a sense of moving toward the unknown. There was also the recognition that to a large extent the managers created the dynamics of the systems themselves. There was the sense that because of an organizational culture comprised of functional silos, authoritarian management, monolithic governance, and inadequate leadership, OsirisCo's managers were little prepared for a takeover. The story, as it turned out, was as much – perhaps much more – about the norms of the old culture as the norms of the new, yet unformed culture. The lack of communication from the acquirer was enhanced by the lack of communication from the acquired. The fear and anxiety experienced were emotions that had been experienced in the pre-acquisition past. Finally, the managers' inabilities to make decisions in the old company were made worse by being acquired by a new company. If the enemy was not entirely us, it was certainly our alter egos!

In the end, the systems thinking group had mixed feelings about their responsibility to convey their findings to new management. Some felt the application of systems thinking to "real" work problems was value enough; others felt it was up to the human resources (HR) members of the group to present the outcome to the new CEO; still others thought it was important to retell the story so that other managers could recognize the takeover as an archetypal event. Everyone in the class, however, could see that something had been missing in their corporate education. They could now see the education that is necessary to prepare for and accommodate change, and the constant need for workplace maintenance in order to destroy fear, raise communication, improve synergy, increase risk, and – oh yes, be profitable!

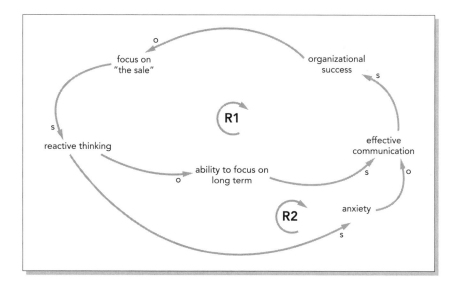

Fig 3.8 Dynamics of focussing on the sale

Summary

I change by not changing at all

What happens when we try to avoid change initiatives

OsirisCo was typical of many organizations that feel they are on the receiving end of an acquisition initiative. OsirisCo had been a good place to work – it had been profitable (a reason that it was acquired), it had been effective (another reason it had been acquired), and it had been a good place to work (a third reason it had been acquired). But when word got out about the impending acquisition, the employees' world began to change. The company suddenly found itself divided in two – people who liked the idea of being acquired, and those who didn't. This set up several dynamics. People began to feel they had lost their sense of trust and respect for the existing management team, and many felt they had been lied to about elements of the acquisition. People began to play games with how they did their jobs – some who felt that their jobs were in jeopardy began to focus on keeping their jobs instead of fulfilling job responsibilities. All these things began to tear the company apart, and, consequently, lessen the ability of the new management to deliver over time.

Had the existing management team been more open about what was going to happen, and why, many of these issues would not have had the impact that they did. When employees do not "see" a future for themselves in a company, they lose interest in the company and begin to lose their effectiveness, both individually and collectively.

Key learning

Always ensure that your employees understand the dynamics of the changes they are going through. This includes why the company is changing in the direction it is, the impact of the changes on the organization as a whole, and the impact on the employees on a personal level.

4

A light at the end of the tunnel
… or an oncoming train?

What happens when we miss the signals telling us where our company is headed

How often has it been heard in organizational meetings that we are, finally, just able to see the "light at the end of the tunnel?" The significance of this statement is usually representative of an organizational dynamic that speaks of hard work, hours of effort, and the desire to accomplish something. But it also speaks of stress, frustration, and the anxiety of not knowing. The use of the metaphor of "the light at the end of the tunnel," although not necessarily providing clarity on which set of dynamics is most prevalent, does provide clarity on the belief that the people who have been putting forth the effort have been relatively in the dark about something – hence the tunnel metaphor.

Once again, we have a story of an organization that has used acquisition as a central growth strategy. DrillCo was facing the challenge of how to implement an organizational-wide software program to bring together all the acquisitions for information reporting and sharing. This implementation initiative was creating pressures on the organization. DrillCo personnel were interviewed during a sharp decline in the energy industry, which was putting additional pressure on the organization.

DrillCo

DrillCo is like many organizations today. It has a solid history, a good workforce, and it is facing many challenges. Among these is how to become a more effective organization in a volatile marketplace. To help accomplish this, DrillCo has undergone several reorganizations as well as beginning to acquire additional business units to complement its core business.

In this move toward hoped-for higher levels of effectiveness, DrillCo has encountered several dynamics – the same dynamics that other organizations have encountered in similar situations. These dynamics have included:

- a sense of lost direction by some employees;
- a feeling of internal competition for control;
- a belief that many parts of the organization do not understand the overall plan to become more effective.

"I think that we are trying to become a bigger company, expanding our services and just trying to be a big company."

"I would assume that we want to become one of the leaders in our industry, diversified in all aspects of the whole industry, but I don't know for sure."

"A lot of people are unsure of what is going on with all these acquisitions, so some of the people are kind of clamming up and not really letting go with how they feel."

"Does management communicate to us very well? I don't think so."

"You know, they are making long-term plans but I am so far down the totem pole and I don't think I am part of their plans."

"Well, I used to feel like I knew something. Now I don't feel like I know anything."

"No, senior management doesn't communicate with us well at all, and with what we are trying to do they should do a better job of it."

"We spend a lot of time trying to understand what we need to understand. This takes too long because we spend time fighting amongst ourselves, fighting changes too."

The feeling that the organization does not appear to know where it is going, or that the direction is not communicated well, combined with the feeling that the employees do not understand how they fit into that picture, is an indication that the organization is not focussed on developing core competencies in its people. This is a demonstration that it is not able to achieve a high level of organizational effectiveness.

The evidence of these dynamics surfaced in a series of interviews with DrillCo personnel, in which internal conflicts over turf and communications gaps occurred. Each of these dynamics has the potential to sidetrack the organization's efforts to implement its technology solution. Additionally, and more importantly, the presence of these dynamics can negatively impact an organization's potential to be viable over time. This became apparent during interviews in which the subject of a fragmented workforce surfaced.

"I know we are all part of DrillCo, but it is not the same out here as at the home office. We used to call ourselves 'stepchildren' because we sometimes felt like that. Being away from the central operation means that we don't get the same information. We are treated differently."

"I think there is a tendency in the acquisitions to develop an 'us versus them' mentality. If you were with DrillCo, you were the us; if you were with one of the acquisitions, you were the them, the ugly stepchild. Our revenues have increased with the acquisitions, but the morale has gone down dramatically."

By beginning to make the overall strategy and the rationale behind it more visible, the employees would be able to "connect" with the strategy and be better able to understand why DrillCo had been moving in the direction it had been moving in. DrillCo management decided to do just that. But like many organizational mistakes, it is not "what" is done that is wrong, it is "how" it is done that causes more problems.

> ● Like many organizational mistakes, it is not "what" is done that is wrong, it is "how" it is done that causes more problems.

DrillCo decided to increase communications by using traditional methods – e-mail, phone messaging, and newsletters. On the surface, this seemed at the time to be a sound idea; by increasing the ways in which communications were circulated throughout the organization, the level of information would increase. At least, that was the idea. The reality was that at DrillCo, there were so many feelings of "separate" communications for different population groups, the additional communications efforts were largely ignored or discounted by the receiving population groups. A good example of "more" not equaling "more effective."

"I am worried that the implementation is going to take too damn long and cost too much. I originally believed it was going to be a $3.5 million project that seems to have gone to $5 million. I also heard that it would take 28 months but now I am told it will only be 18 months. I don't think so."

"The implementation of a new software package will impact my job, not as far as eliminating my job or anything because somebody will have to have the key information for management to be able to analyze any stuff, but my job sure will be different, and nobody is telling me how."

"I think that this ERP (enterprise resource planning) system that is coming will result in a lot of good changes, but I think it will be different for everyone."

"If they don't implement it right the first time, then there will be a lot of trouble."

In any organization, there are two types of news – good news and bad news. I have come to believe that the only bad news is the news that we don't have access to. Knowing something that we would normally say is "bad news" is not as bad as "not knowing" at all. Not knowing leads to assumptions, rumors, and fractionalization of employees and their efforts. Differing assumptions, rumors, and fractionalization of an employee group can lead to a dynamic known as "gaming the system." Gaming the system is a reference to "doing what you do but in a way that can be self-serving."

One of the rules of system dynamics is "structure drives behavior." In the case of organizations, the behaviors include those of the employees. The structures are policies and procedures, mental models, and stated goals that an organization develops over time. Policies and procedures include both the explicit (policy manuals and procedural manuals) and the implicit (how things really get done). Although policy and procedural manuals are developed to help guide an employee through the organizational maze, in most organizations the manuals describe the "hard" way to get things done, and over time an easier, less cumbersome set of methods is usually developed by employees.

As each employee wrestles with the structures, one of several things can happen: they can adapt to the needs of the organization directly, they can adapt the organization's needs to their willingness and ability to satisfy them, or they can simply leave the organization. The first could be called employee commitment, the second could be called gaming the system. In the case of DrillCo, many of the employees chose to game the system.

Gaming the system is something that happens in an organization when the structures that have been formally put in place make it difficult to meet the goals by using the explicit policies and procedures, or so the employees believe. By "flexing" the policies and procedures, employees are able to ensure that they can continue to work in an environment in which they are rewarded for the work that they do. However, by "flexing" the policies and procedures, the employees are doing little more than modifying or short-circuiting the system that is supposed to ensure organizational effectiveness. In the case of DrillCo, gaming the system occurred on several levels, and the activity was largely due to the combination of the growth strategy and the plans to implement the technology solution as a lever for the strategy.

With the stated goal of the organization being the successful implementation of the "new" technology solution, it quickly became apparent that the solution was another problem looming for the employees. After several years getting used to the existing computer system, they were now told they would once again have to change the way they did business. Changing the way in which data was collected and disseminated had been a major problem for DrillCo collectively, as it was individually. To overcome the looming problem, DrillCo management decided to put an incentive program in place. The incentives were designed to ensure that the employees most affected by the new system would readily "absorb" the system into their daily work life.

With the onset of the new system, organizational personnel began to explore how they could game the computer system incentive structure. At meetings in which management would disseminate information regarding the new system, local managers – those who would be held accountable for the successful implementation of the new system – were given the procedures that would be required. Additionally, they were given information about how the implementation process would be monitored and measured, as well as details about the incentive program structure. The measures were numerical targets such as amount of data that would be expected to be inputed into the new system on a daily basis, timeliness of the data input, and accuracy of the input process. To game this program, all that needed to be done was to ensure that a sufficient amount of data was keyed in daily, on time, and accurately. If this was done, managers would receive their financially driven awards. The unintended consequence of this structure, and the thing that enabled the gaming, was the disconnection between what was input and what relevance it had to the organization. Managers became very adept at ensuring that they had all the data they needed for their local sites, but were able to neglect key information that could have been utilized by the central office for more effective planning to reduce duplication of services and waste – the reason that the system had been purchased in the first place.

Incentive-based gaming

There are several ways in which employees can game a system. Gaming a reward or incentive system is one of them. A unit of the United States government was trying to reduce the overall cost of procurement. While exploring various ways to accomplish this, they determined that putting in a set of incentives for the people who were responsible for purchasing should increase the potential for major cost savings. The incentive program worked, at least from the metric of the number of incentives paid out. The cost savings identified were substantial, but the savings that were identified were only on paper, and only on the surface. The long-term overall costs were actually increasing. By looking at the incentive program through the lens of systems thinking, it became clear that the employees were managing the dollars involved to achieve the incentives, while the savings that were supposed to generate the incentives were not there (*see* Fig 4.1).

As can be seen in the systemically developed diagram, there were two ways to deal with the total cost overruns – by managing the dollars, or by managing the system. By implementing incentives – in this case, cash incentives to those who could produce the desired savings levels – the government unit was asking people to focus their efforts on managing the dollars, not the system itself. By looking at the loops, we can see that as total cost overruns increased, the more management of dollars went on. This was supposed to decrease the total cost overruns. The other option would have been to focus employees' efforts on managing the system. This too would reduce the total cost overruns over time. But with the implementation of a system of cash-based incentives, the employees became addicted to gaming the system – producing paper savings to obtain the incentives – and this would pre-empt any possibility of ever managing the system. This actually

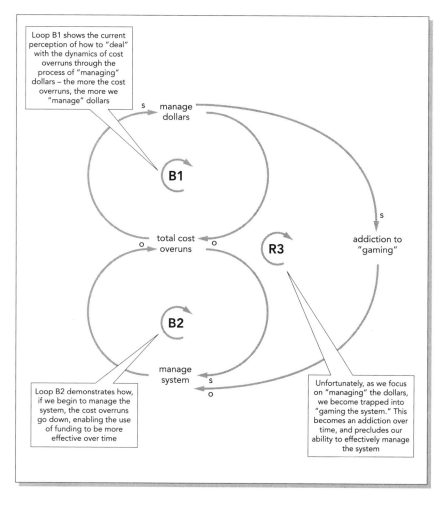

Loop B1 shows the current perception of how to "deal" with the dynamics of cost overruns through the process of "managing" dollars – the more the cost overruns, the more we "manage" dollars

s manage dollars

B1

total cost overuns
o   o

R3

addiction to "gaming"
s

B2

manage system   s
o

Loop B2 demonstrates how, if we begin to manage the system, the cost overruns go down, enabling the use of funding to be more effective over time

Unfortunately, as we focus on "managing" the dollars, we become trapped into "gaming the system." This becomes an addiction over time, and precludes our ability to effectively manage the system

Fig 4.1 The addiction of managing the dollars

aggravated the overall system, which was not designed to be cost effective, only responsive to potential government service demands.

To better understand what was going on in the government agency, it became critical to look at the entire cost-reduction program systemically to determine which elements of the program were structural in nature and which were event oriented. Structural variables are those that can create organizational behaviors over time. Event variables are those that are the result of the behaviors over time. Structural variables include the explicit and implicit policies and procedures, mental models, stated goals, and physical layout. The incentives that had been developed had a short-term perspective and did not take into consideration current organizational structures – the explicit and implicit policies and procedures, and mental models – they were all nothing more than another set of stated goals; to save money.

How the savings were to be achieved was never made explicit, nor how the savings would be measured. The incentives fell into several categories: accountability for savings, recognition for savings achieved, compensation, and metrics that identified immediate savings. These incentive metrics all related to specific events – things that would be highly visible and immediate in nature. By following the new incentive program, employees would "win." By not following the incentive program, employees believed they would be passed over for promotion, lose funding for departmental efforts, and risk the impact of a culture that was focussed on the short term. These perceived negative impacts are all structural in nature, and are, structurally, disincentives. **When designing initiatives and organizational programs designed to achieve specific organizational goals, it is important to ensure that the incentives to "buy in" to the program are structural in nature, not based on events that can result in overall losses.**

Alignment mismatch gaming

When there is a mismatch between the stated organizational mission and purpose and the perceived belief of what it is on the part of the employees, there is a high risk of organizational gaming the system. DrillCo had been growing at a relatively fast rate for several years, largely fueled through acquisitions. The rationale behind this growth strategy was quite easy to understand – by identifying organizations that had substantial revenue streams, it could acquire them and, therefore, become a larger organization without having to deal with the constraints of time. After several years of growing in this manner, many employees began to adopt the belief that the mission and purpose of DrillCo was not to conduct its core business in the energy industry but to acquire other organizations.

> When there is a mismatch between the stated organizational mission and purpose and the perceived belief of what it is on the part of the employees, there is a high risk of organizational gaming the system.

This belief that growing by acquisition was more important than simply growing was not made explicit. What began to happen was that key decision makers started to shift their decision processes to focus on how they could posture the company for another acquisition as opposed to ensuring the long-term sustainability of the organization through effective management. This shift in thinking began to change the focus of the employees, for it became clear to them that the stated goals of the company were not the same as the activities being acted out by the management team.

In Fig 4.2, we can begin to see the impact of gaming the system in an organization where there is a mismatch between the explicit mission and the perceived, or implicit, mission. The structure identified by the figure in loops B1 and B2 shows the dynamics that are apparent on two levels – the level of stated mission and purpose (B1) and the level of perceived mission and purpose (B2). As these two dynamics support each other, the overall organizational performance increases. However, individually they begin to exhibit adversarial tendencies, i.e. as the focus of organizational efforts shifts from service (the stated mission) to acquisitions (the perceived mission), it causes a shift in thinking about the importance and concern about operational issues that can impact the core business. This tends to create an adversarial relationship between different population groups within the organization. Gaming the system occurs when organizational personnel see the shift, or simply believe that there has been a shift in thinking from the stated mission to a focus on acquisitions as the key strategy for the company.

Figure 4.3 shows the shift in beliefs from the past environment to the current environment in DrillCo. This shift is a distinct decrease in the level of alignment in thinking regarding organizational climate. This is a function of the fact that employees had begun to game the system – one that was designed and built around the energy industry service sector – to be able to "exist" and demonstrate either real or perceived effectiveness in a system that was implicitly focussed on something other than the core business.

Gaming the system occurs when personal reward systems and structures become more attractive than organizational rewards; when there is little organizational alignment regarding the mission and purpose of the organization; and when the existing infrastructure is not adequate to support organizational activities that are expected of the employees.

In a debrief of the interview process for senior management of DrillCo, an interesting dynamic arose. While discussing the lack of alignment and organizational behaviors due to perceived disconnections between stated goals and what appeared to be the implicit beliefs of many of the employees, a senior vice-president of DrillCo spoke up. He said that this disconnection,

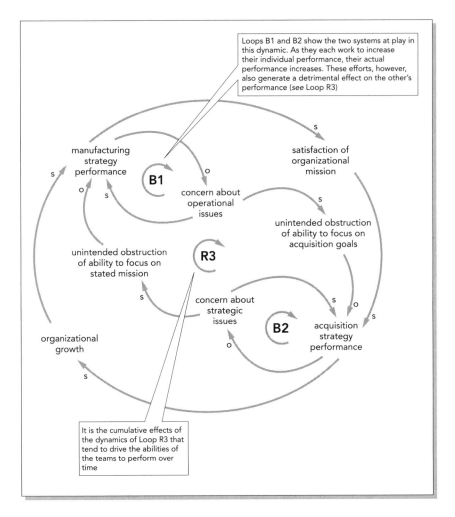

Fig 4.2 The impact of gaming the system in an organization where there is a mismatch between the explicit and the implicit mission

and the associated less-than-effective behaviors, were not surprising to him as he had known for many years about the problems that my research was "discovering." When asked why he had done nothing about resolving them, his response was: "Maybe I like the organization like this." This comment, which apparently came as a shock to the other members of the senior management team, sends several signals:

● there is a mismatch between the stated goals of the organization and the implicit goals;

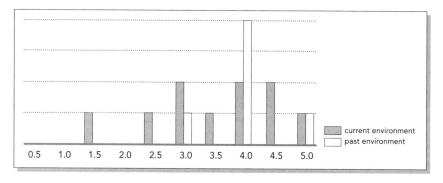

Fig 4.3 Level of alignment regarding organizational community

- there is a mismatch between the beliefs of the organizational personnel of what is most important for the organization to focus on;
- there is a sense that an amount of chaos is acceptable within the organization;
- if members of the senior management team condone chaos and reduced effectiveness due to the chaos and gaps in beliefs, the organization overall will not become effective over time.

To offset the effects of these signals, there are several things that can be done:

- facilitate conversations with company personnel based on the causal loop diagrams that identify the dynamics at play in the organization. This will both increase understanding of what is going on, and help to build alignment. These conversations should be with senior, mid-level, and line managers;
- determine whether to focus efforts on changing the system to eliminate gaming, or eliminate the perceived need to game the system. The latter can be accomplished by examining the scope of the gap between how the organization is supposed to work, and how it actually works;
- develop a work plan to deploy throughout the organization, ensuring that representatives from all areas of the organization have a clear understanding of what needs to be done, how it will be accomplished, and why. Check the anticipated work plan effects with the structural causal loop diagrams for validity.

Summary

A light at the end of the tunnel ... or an oncoming train?

What happens when we miss the signals telling us where our company is headed

DrillCo had had its ups and downs, in the same way as most organizations that are tied to a volatile industry like the energy industry. To ensure the company's ability to be sustainable over time, DrillCo management decided to begin acquiring similar companies. And to help assimilate these companies into one cohesive organization, the management team decided to implement a technology system that would "connect" all the business units. On the surface, it seemed like a good idea. But as we have seen so many times, it was not "what" the company was trying to do that was wrong, it was "how" it was trying to do it. This set up a dynamic where many of the employees – both line employees and middle management employees – began to game the system. They began to focus on how to circumvent the new technology system instead of focussing on how to use the system as a business tool to become more effective. Over time, gaming the system created the exact opposite effect to that which management had wanted or expected.

Gaming the system is a real tragedy in companies, for it exhausts resources, reduces effectiveness, and kills any positive organizational culture that might have existed. Gaming the system can be reduced or eliminated, but it requires the efforts of management to make this happen. By making system gaming visible as an issue, by focussing on its root causes, and by getting and sharing feedback, the impact of gaming can be reduced and eliminated. This can give the company back its energy to focus on delivering high-quality products and services to its customers – what every company wants.

Key learning

To create lasting organizational change through the implementation of technology requires changes in organizational behaviors. Always ensure that your employees are able to see the implications of the decisions of both management and themselves. Make sure that employees do not perceive that the company is developing initiatives that are not targetted to add value to the company and the employees themselves.

5

Next time, let's just solve the problem of world hunger

What happens when project scope creeps out of control

In some companies, goals seem to simply come out of the air. Stated goals are a component of organizational structures, and it is the structures in organizations that tend to drive organizational behaviors. When the goals have the appearance of being derived from vapor, it can provoke a set of behaviors that can be detrimental to the long-term sustainability of an organization. This chapter explores how parts of one particular organization were impacted by such a situation.

Most companies' goals and objectives result from a strategy development process. In the case of WireCo, however, some goals seemed to simply evolve, or perhaps more appropriately, just appear. One of the senior WireCo managers had been in a meeting of stock analysts and was asked what he thought his company's earnings would be for the next fiscal year. When he gave his assumption of what they would be, the analyst responded by saying, "Hmmm, we thought they would be higher." The response was not, "those earnings are not good," nor was it, "isn't there some way in which you can achieve higher earnings?" It was simply a comment that reflected the analyst's assumption of what the earnings would be. This comment set in motion a series of dynamics that would be the beginning of a cultural shift in the company.

Shortly after the meeting, the senior manager returned to the organization's main office and called a meeting of his direct reports – all unit presidents and senior managers. At this meeting, it was determined that, to ensure that the company's earnings would be higher – to a level that most would believe was set arbitrarily – the organization would begin a process in which it could reduce the amount of funds spent with outside vendors. The goal was to produce the savings by a targetted date, by which time the organization would be able to demonstrate higher earnings prior to another stock analysts meeting.

The process that was used made sense, on the surface: involve employees from all the business units to focus on two things – identify areas for savings, and reduce the expenditures in those areas. This effort validated the belief that it is rarely "what" an organization does that is wrong, it is most often "how" an organization does what it does that causes the most problems, both in the short term and the long term. This case clearly demonstrated that it was the process used to achieve the savings that had detrimental effects on the organization's ability to be effective over time.

WireCo

WireCo, another "growth through acquisition" organization, was coming under great pressure. Or so management believed. One of the senior members of the WireCo management team had had a meeting with several Wall Street analysts, and although he was able to show how the company's earnings had increased dramatically over the previous year, he was told that the analysts had expected more. He brought this news back to the company along with the implicit message that the company had better improve in the next year or there would be massive problems – an example of how subtle messages from external sources can change an organization's focus.

It was decided at the most senior levels that WireCo would immediately begin a process of reducing the money it spent with external vendors. This was an ambitious goal, and once again on the surface, its efforts were wildly successful. However, underlying this success was an undercurrent of pain that would lead to more pain in the future. This pain was largely due to the lack of focus on the part of the organization on effectively communicating the project vision, creating an environment of understanding, and thinking systemically about the long-term ramifications of these actions.

"The big picture, the way I see it, is that we made some promises a year or two ago when we acquired another company. We said that we were going to have all kinds of synergies, cost reductions, and great earnings projections. We have not seen some of those promises out there and we have got to cut back on some expenditures to meet some earnings projections."

"It felt like they were stretched goals, which was a demotivator. I don't believe in stretch goals that are stretched to the point that they cause stress because when you are stressed to the point of working on a goal that is unobtainable, it just creates a lot of tension that is not necessary. That doesn't encourage originality, it doesn't encourage innovation, it doesn't encourage thinking in the company's best interests."

"I would say that when we started this project there was a high level degree of skepticism on the part of some business units that there was anything to be achieved by this."

"It was frustrating because it was so political and because everyone on the team wasn't on board, so that made it harder."

By setting high expectations, perhaps higher than could be achieved in most environments, the organization had set itself up for a potential problem that then set the stage for the gap in expectation achievement, as well as becoming a potential organizational demotivator.

> ● When an organization grows through acquisition, one of the most important variables that can impact its long-term success is the ability to acculturate the employees of the newly acquired business unit into the existing organizational culture.

When an organization grows through acquisition, one of the most important variables that can impact its long-term success is the ability to acculturate the employees of the newly acquired business unit into the existing organizational culture. This potential inability to acculturate employees is impacted additionally by the level and type of existing organizational culture. In the case of WireCo, this dynamic played heavily on its cost reduction project efforts.

"They (one of the business units) probably have the strongest, most ingrained and entrenched cultures of any of the companies."

"We had run numbers of teams before and had gotten various results and so many philosophies of how best to use them. The conclusion here was, let's dedicate folks

more or less full-time to this team assignment, but only for a short period of time. The idea was to get in and get it done and get out of there."

It was decided to assemble sets of teams which would be charged with the identification and development of cost-reduction areas that would yield the desired target results, in this case millions of dollars. The strategy of utilizing internal teams of employees seemed to be a sound idea – who better to identify the areas for savings than the employees who had expertise in specific functional organizational areas? Using internal teams is usually recommended as an effective way to achieve buy-in for cost-reduction efforts, as it tends to eliminate the belief that those higher up are making all the decisions, both on strategic and operational levels. In the case of WireCo, it was clear that the senior management team was setting the strategic direction, but that they were looking to the employees to help set the operational direction.

> ● The strategy of utilizing internal teams of employees seemed to be a sound idea – who better to identify the areas for savings than the employees who had expertise in specific functional organizational areas?

Pulling together sets of teams (in the case of WireCo, the number of teams was in excess of 12, all to be running concurrently) can be done in several ways. But just as in the ConnectCo case study, WireCo decided to appoint people to serve on the teams. Drafting in people to perform jobs that they may or may not have expertise for, or care to do, or are paid to do, can result in dynamics that can be detrimental to team outcomes. Those dynamics began to surface at WireCo.

"I would love to tell you that I waved a flag and said, 'pick me, pick me' (for the team) though that wasn't really the case."

"With the amount of commitment to the team and the existing workload, the level of stress was unbelievable."

The issue of existing job responsibilities and who would fulfill them became an issue that may have mitigated the sense of accomplishment on the part of many team members. Although the teams did identify savings that surpassed the targets, many team members felt their efforts were not appreciated. After all, it was the team members who had "gone the extra mile" for the organization by not only working their "real jobs" but participating on the teams as well.

"Who took care of the work I couldn't get done? The ones who will probably not be recognized for making sure that this thing worked."

"Would I do it again? No, absolutely not. I did 12 weeks and in no way did they relieve any of my normal workload. I did all my work at night, 16–18-hour days for weeks."

"We met four days a week, every week, for 16 weeks. We did our real jobs after work, at night."

"I am sure that some people at points were very stressed – I'm convinced of that."

"Were people on the teams demonstrating stress? Absolutely, without fail."

"It never came into my head in the sense that someone was saying, 'I can't be on this project any more because I've got too much to do.' We certainly had situations where we had some people who weren't able to attend meetings because they felt they had a lot to do. When that happened, someone would call the oversight committee member of that company and they would get things pulled off their plates and give it to other people."

"We were more results and goals oriented than we were emotional, feeling oriented. We were given a commitment that we would have the resources we needed and we made a commitment to deliver."

The sense of frustration due to stress and pressure for results began to take its toll on many of the team members long before the completion of the project. Much of that stress and pressure stemmed from the apparent lack of back-up support for team members. To believe that the expectation is to spend many hours every day for quite a few weeks while still being required to complete the existing job requirements can be draining, both physically and emotionally. This implicit pressure, coupled with the explicit expectation of a "due date" for the project deliverable of cost savings, resulted in a sense of demoralization on the part of many team members.

"For me, there were late hours and weekends. Fortunately, I have a very capable assistant and she was able to carry the ball on a lot of things that I normally would have done. It was really a challenge and I am still catching up."

"I am not sure, but I think that the teams, for the most part, spent about two days a week on this project – eight hours per day. There was lip service paid to the stress level, and other people would help, but I'm sure it came out of those people's hides."

"It was very demanding time-wise, and it was frustrating in the sense that it was a difficult project to do in a short period of time."

By the time the project was completed, the numbers had been hit, and without a doubt this created a sense of success in the minds of most of the employees. But the success, or more appropriately the perception of success, was a function of the explicit goals – in this case, to identify and develop an amount of potential savings through cost reduction.

"There is a difference between savings on paper and savings after implementation. Those are two different things."

"Some of the savings weren't as good in reality as they were on paper."

"I am not sure that all the savings that we developed will be realized. We will not know right away, but will have to wait for after the implementation to see if it will happen."

"I don't think that we will be able to implement all the recommendations, but I also think that some of the figures are conservative, so we will probably realize 100 percent of the dollars. The main problem will be the implementation. I know that the team had lots and lots of controversy and implementation issues associated with the project, so I'm not sure if those issues are going to be resolved to get the benefits."

"I'm going to guess that we will only see about 60 percent of the savings, and I am talking about real dollars and cents. Real savings can only come from hard dollars, and some of these savings were soft dollars. Besides, the biggest problem will be in the implementation process."

At the end of the project cycle, each team was able to present their findings to senior management, and to hear the senior managers say thank you for their efforts. At the time of the presentations, it became clear that the management team that was responsible for the project was relatively unaware of the level of frustration and stress felt by team members due to workload saturation. To their credit, the management team did express their thanks in a very positive way, but there were mixed feelings on the part of the team members after their presentations. Some of this related to being told "thank you" for putting in an effort that was, in their words, "clearly above and beyond the call of duty," while at the same time it was believed that the managers who were verbally thanking them would be receiving large financial bonuses based on the potential savings that the teams had developed.

The key learning opportunities that came from the work with WireCo can be grouped into issues relating to three core competencies: vision, understanding, and systemic thinking.

Vision

It was obvious that the vision of the project was not made explicitly clear. There were some of the senior management team who disputed this, but that conflict was due mainly to their belief that the visibility of the financial savings target was all that the teams needed to know. It could be argued that the goal was not to simply cut costs. Some believed that the underlying goal was to accomplish two things: to increase the potential of the organization to become more viable over time due to high debt levels, and to create the perception in the minds of stock analysts that the organization could become more profitable in a short period of time. The first was long-term thinking, but as a result of short-term thinking. The second was clearly short-term thinking, period. Having an organization react to the perceptions of external analysts can create dynamics that begin to reinforce the belief that the organization can accommodate external demands, a belief that can become addictive over time. As a result, it might spawn initiatives that are not in the best long-term interests of the organization. Regardless of the real or perceived reasons for the project, i.e. the vision for the project, the very fact that there was not high alignment in the purpose of the goal would lead one to believe that the organization had not communicated the vision well.

Always ensure that everyone involved directly and indirectly in a project clearly understands the purpose, rationale, and goals of the project.

Understanding

The core competency of understanding was not supported well through the project. Understanding, as a competency, relates to the ability to listen empathically, to truly understand what is important, and why. The comments relating to stress and workload were largely unheard by senior management, although they had been raised repeatedly. This may have been due to a variety of reasons, including the perception on the part of those who communicated it (mid-level managers and external facilitators) that this type of message would be received as a signal that the onsite project managers were not capable of completing their assigned tasks of managing the project. It could have been due to the fact that the message was never explicitly sent, i.e. team members did not openly express their concerns to their direct superiors, or it may simply not have been heard by those who could have changed the environment. Regardless of the reason, exercising the competency of understanding could have reduced or eliminated many of the negative feelings about the project and the way that senior management handled it.

> ● Exercising the competency of understanding could have reduced or eliminated many of the negative feelings about the project and the way that senior management handled it.

Always ensure that all employees involved in project teams, and those who manage them, agree to have an open environment, one that encourages feedback from anyone to anyone.

Systemic thinking

Systemic thinking was not used as effectively as it could have been during this project.

"One of my concerns about this project was that it necessarily focussed on short-term savings – we needed results now and that is how the teams were constructed."

"Maybe the next step would be a more sophisticated sort of discussion and analysis, cost modeling, and the like. There simply wasn't time for it in this exercise and as a result, it seemed that the results that were delivered will cause us to bypass savings that are grander in future years."

"I'm a little concerned that saying, 'let's look at the inefficiencies, let's get our earnings per share to whatever,' is just fixing to fail over time. I would like to look at the true problem and understand what it is and then solve it. That is looking at the organization from a bigger perspective."

"I realize the bottom line of the project was to cut cost, but with a closed focus, you are going to end up with not as good of results as if we could have tackled the real problem."

Always look at both the short and long-term ramifications of project team efforts. In many cases, a short-term solution only leads to a long-term problem.

By most accounts, the WireCo project was successful. But the real success of this and other projects undertaken by WireCo will only be truly judged over time. Not three months, not six months, not twelve months, but perhaps over years. And the true measure of success of this and other projects will not be determined solely by financial metrics.

Summary

Let's just solve the problem of world hunger

What happens when the project scope creeps out of control

WireCo is one of those companies whose management team has the best of intentions but sometimes loses sight of the big picture, so that the intentions get misplaced. The management team, or more appropriately one of the senior managers of the company, heard something, and without spending time to validate what was said, or even more importantly what the words actually meant, decided to "take action." Taking action before understanding is a kind of modified, "ready, aim, shoot" concept. In this case, in hindsight, even the management team believe it might have been "ready, shoot, aim." When hearing that a stock analyst had expected that WireCo's earnings would be higher, the senior manager convinced the rest of the senior management team that the company should develop a project to reduce the amount of money it spent with external vendors. On the surface this seemed rational, but once again it was not what was done that was a problem, it was how it was done that caused the difficulties.

A group of teams was assembled to figure out how to reduce this external spending, and after many months of work it did just that. But the price that was paid for the savings was immense. The company culture took a major hit, largely due to the inability of the project team members to balance their new responsibilities with their old ones. Once again it is a story of too little communication too late, if at all; of mixed signals from management, including signals that were never sent.

Key learning

Always ensure before management decisions are implemented, that they are not based on short-term thinking. Employees have an incredibly high level of capacity to "see" through initiatives that will not add lasting value to the company. Additionally, make sure that employees feel that the extra effort they extend to the company is not in vain, that they are appreciated, and consequently that they are rewarded by management.

6

Like so many dominoes in a row

What happens when things begin to get out of control

The domino effect is an example of inductive reasoning. To "prove" that each domino in a line will fall requires only two things – that all the dominoes are lined up with the same spatial relationship between them as the first two, and that the first domino, when tipped, will knock over the second domino. When this happens, it is clear that all the other dominoes will fall as well.

Although we intuitively understand this concept, we tend to forget the effect when considering organizational behaviors. An organizational environment is much like the spatial relationship between a row of dominoes. Each person has a distinct relationship with the others in the organization. Some of these relationships are quite clear, while others, although connected through the organizational matrix, are not as well defined. When for some reason some are impacted by organizational behaviors that are not conducive for building an increased level of effectiveness, it is typical that the others in the organization become impacted in the same way. If we understand this concept of the domino effect, it is interesting that we forget to apply it to the dynamics that are associated with organizational behaviors.

Imagine an organization that is undergoing tremendous accelerated growth due to the concerted efforts of senior management. Some of the effects of this growth include a reduced ability to focus on what is important and instead focus on what is urgent, increased stress, and reduced productivity. When these things begin to impact some in the organization, the overall outcome on an organizational level is the same – a reduced ability to focus on what is important and instead focus on what is urgent, increased stress, and reduced productivity. So what traditionally happens in an organization that is experiencing this dynamic? The senior management simply cranks it up some more. More of the same will lead to more of the same – the domino effect.

WestCo

WestCo is unlike many companies – in the organization's history, it has consistently been able to achieve and surpass its goals, for both revenue and growth. In this case, however, success has had a price attached to it. In the past three years, WestCo has grown from a 17-person organization to one in excess of 160 people, and with an expected headcount increase of more than 30 percent in 2000. And this is not a high-tech dot com.

To keep up with all the changes in the organizational structure and the increased demands on management, the senior managers at WestCo embarked on an initiative to improve leadership within the organization. They decided to bring in an external group to help facilitate the professional development capabilities of their people in five areas, all identified as leadership capabilities. The capabilities identified were: effective communications, making decisions, developing relationships, building ownership, and creating vision. The dynamics experienced by WestCo during this initiative were interesting from a research standpoint for some of the issues and dynamics that the managers were trying to avoid through the initiative to build their leadership capacity were the very things that kept them from achieving what they set out to do.

From the very beginning, WestCo's growth had been driven by a few senior people who not only could see the vision for the future but were the ones who developed it. In the process of growing the business, the ability to ensure that all new employees were in alignment with that vision diminished, if for no other reason than the sheer volume of new people. The leadership team believed they had to make the decision whether to work on the deployment of the vision or to work on the development of the business itself. Even though these two choices needn't be exclusive, the team chose to build the business and put together a wider leadership project team to look at how to build the leadership capacity of the company. From the outset of the project, there were questions regarding the make-up of the team and its direction.

"There are several questions I have around the team. Okay? Do we still agree with the direction? Is that the right five things that we need? If it is right for us, how do we know when it is done? And how do we get the feedback to know that what we're putting in is getting us to the place we want to get?"

"Right now, we don't know how to make decisions as a group. We don't have rules about how to do that. We don't have rules on how to communicate, when to communicate up and when to communicate down. For example, a couple of weeks ago, there were a series of decisions made by different people in the organization that cost us a lot. And they were never communicated up the chain in a fashion that we (as senior managers) would have wanted them to be. We found ourselves scrambling because we were trying to fix something that's really broken – decisions that someone made in a vacuum that had unintended consequences in other places. And probably, had it moved up the chain a little bit, one of us could have said, 'ah, but wait! If you do that, you will end up with this.' But it was a decision that was made in a vacuum. Things like that have to be fixed. It's just like the foundation of a house, and I don't want to build this house and not have the foundation."

"I'm looking forward to just getting a real clear alignment, as clear as we can get in terms of what pieces we want, how we want to go about it, and beginning to put together the model, the schedule, and the execution."

"I do feel like we're operating on quicksand."

"It seems our context is that we are moving from hierarchical to network. We have to get a common understanding of what the situation is."

"It was the phenomenal growth and our inability to get everybody up to speed quick enough that pushed the beginning (of this project). There were and still are a lot of growing pains on all levels."

"It's a good thing we are doing it. There are some really fantastic things going on here, but our ability to learn quickly was next to zero."

"When you have to go to the outside to get enough people to manage, there is a risk that they won't be prepared to hit the ground running."

"Some of the people we have acquired may not fit, but we need to recognize who they are and what it will take to get everybody who remains up to the needed level of management skill."

Although the level of alignment in the group was relatively high, the highest area of alignment revolved around the belief that there was little alignment in the collective vision and deployment process for disseminating the vision throughout the larger organization. From the beginning, WestCo's growth had been driven through a strategy that appeared to center on selling and hiring, i.e. get some work and then get some people to do the work, then get some more work and get some more people. A key element in utilizing this strategy is the ability of the people who are hired to be effective in a very short period of time, which would imply hiring experienced people.

Hiring people with experience is a great strategy. The rationale makes sense – to decrease the "get them up and running" learning curve, hire people who have already done similar work. Well, it sounds good on paper. Any time an employee group undergoes a change, there is a delay in them achieving the desired level of effectiveness. This delay, known as the "double-J" or "valley of despair," arises because it takes time for a population to be able to learn something new, and then more time before they are able to effectively use that learning. Hiring experienced people from other organizations is not really any different than training existing employees in new methods and techniques. Experienced hires may have experience, but most likely not in the same system and structure as that of a new employer.

> ● Hiring experienced people from other organizations is not really any different than training existing employees in new methods and techniques.

The initial dip in the level of effectiveness (*see* Fig 6.1) is largely due to the time it takes to learn the "what" of the new system, i.e. "I have done this type of work, but never in this system. What do I do here?" The second dip is due to the time it takes to learn the "how" and "why" of the new system, i.e. "how do I maneuver through this new system?" and "why is this important in this organization?" By hiring experienced people with the belief that they would be up and running sooner than new hires, it was possible that the management team was deluding itself. This is rarely the case. The depth and breadth of the dips in the graph may vary, but they will always be present. Learning takes time, whether it is learning new software, new methodologies, new client approaches, or how a management system

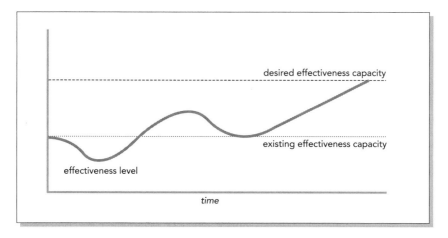

Fig 6.1 The level of effectiveness over time

works. Patience, at least to some degreee, is needed. An appropriate question might be, "Do we have, or will we have, enough patience to survive the dip in effectiveness before we get to where we want to be?"

Simply ensuring that WestCo had enough people to keep up with the demands to meet sales goals was the greatest problem that the leadership team thought they had in the early years. Ensuring that the employees were able to "know" both what to do and "why" to do it became an even bigger issue as the organization grew. This was the difference between single-loop learning and double-loop learning.

In many organizations, including WestCo, it is the structures of the organization that create the greatest obstacles to achieving high levels of understanding. The structures include the implicit and explicit policies and procedures, the mental models of the employees, and the stated goals of the company. This was no different at WestCo.

"Our biggest weakness is communication and setting the structure for the group. There is no direction setting and there's not really a lot of leadership from the top coming down. I think it is because they are too busy with all the customer work. It's growing so fast that we haven't had the time to take a step back and look at how we need to structure."

"One of our weaknesses is that we have the desire to help coach and train and support new individuals, but I don't know that we actually do this in real life. The issue here is time – we don't have enough of it."

"We have a group of people who are pretty competent and know what we are doing, but then we get overloaded because we end up taking on all the new development and all that kind of stuff. That leaves us with not a whole lot of time to be able to support new people coming into the organization who need information on kind of a just-in-time basis."

"Frequently, when I need information, they are too busy to give it to me or they send me to someone who really doesn't have it."

"Sometimes you can get your hands on information right away, and sometimes you can spend hours sort of fruitlessly groping for something."

"I think we put up some pretty serious roadblocks for our people sometimes."

"The communication lines are terrible, both going up and going down. That's the biggest problem. I get feedback coming down, but it's not the right feedback. It is not understanding what is happening down here so it pops up in little places going, 'Ooooh, what are you talking about? We have been doing that for months.' I think that the top levels don't have a handle on what is really happening, the real details of it."

"Some of our managers don't take feedback well. It depends on the manager, but some are better than others. They are not all open to feedback and some aren't responsive. I think that a lot of it has to do with the level of experience. Some of our managers are inexperienced and they feel that it is a reflection on them if the feedback to them is not perfect. I think that everyone is so afraid that perfection won't be achieved without the boss seeing."

Additional dynamics at play in the organization began to surface when the project team started to meet. Some of these dynamics were well known by the employees, while some of the new employees appeared to be unaware of them, at least until they had actually been on the job. Organizational dynamics are like the wind – you can't see it, but you sure can feel it when it blows over you.

> ● Organizational dynamics are like the wind – you can't see it, but you sure can feel it when it blows over you.

The dynamics were largely structural in nature, and their impact was to create problems for both the team and the team's objective of increasing the leadership capacity of the organization. This is an important point: the senior management of the organization were well aware of the gap between the current reality of leadership and the desired level of leadership capability and were trying to do something about it. However, due to some of the implicit structures in place in the organization – structures that the senior management were aware of – the project team's ability to deal with the gap was to be severely diminished. One of the biggest reasons for this was the belief on the part of the senior management that they themselves had not created or reinforced the gap. This was a misconception on their part for in most cases it is the senior management that do just that.

"I just try to keep up with the growth and all the changes."

"We spend so much time firefighting. We get stuck spending all our time in reactive mode instead of being proactive."

"I think our communication is what is holding us back. It's a big hole right now and it is hurting us."

"We kind of went away from our management meetings because I think that we felt they were taking too much time and they weren't productive. I'm not sure, you would have to ask the people who decided that."

"I don't think that everyone can go to the owners and say, 'Hey, we have a big communication gap here.' I am not sure that they would believe it. Let me rephrase that: it would depend who you are. It would depend on the person giving the message."

"I guess I wonder how we can change an environment that has a management or leadership that aren't willing to change themselves."

"They are trying to facilitate, without driving, our new management team so we can deal with the growth we have. Sometimes it can be frustrating because we appear to be heading in a direction that we don't understand at the time, but when we finally see where we are going and why, it doesn't seem to make sense."

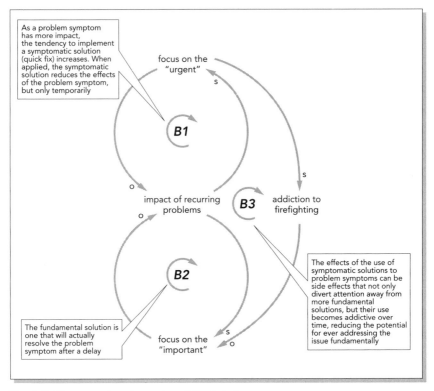

Fig 6.2 The negative dynamics of firefighting

Summary

Like so many dominoes in a row

What happens when things begin to get out of control

WestCo is one of those companies that has grown through investment in its people, not through acquisition and merger policies. By almost every measure, the company has been very successful – increased headcount, increased revenues, increased opportunities. But its very success was also its failure. To ensure that it could continue to grow at the rate that it had, WestCo senior management decided to increase its middle-management capacity to lead. What an admirable thing to do. But in the process of doing this, it became apparent that much of its success was at a terrible price. WestCo's middle management was suffering from lack of understanding, lack of vision, and lack of ability to think systemically. And it was this lack of core skills that began to reverse the gains that had been made. So many of the internal structures in the organization – the explicit and implicit policies and procedures, the mental models, and the stated goals – were driving behaviors that manifested themselves in burnout, stress, and lack of ability to sustain success over time.

Key learning

When your organization is undergoing tremendous growth, especially through acquisition or merger, ensure that there is a process in place that will help employees from acquired companies assimilate into a new culture. Having to deal with assimilation after the fact can result in lost opportunities, wasted resources, and fractionalization of efforts. Changing behaviors is the key to an effective assimilation effort as part of the process of merger or acquisition.

7

Is the steering bad or is it just the driver?

What happens when management becomes more important than leadership

Management in most organizations have a common belief – the belief in the "rightness" of their decisions. This belief is reinforced every time a new manager is appointed to run a department, a division, or an entire organization. The belief comes from the very fact that the person has been chosen to make the decisions that will impact the organization – and that they have been chosen over someone else.

What a marvelous reinforcement this is. "I must be the best, for I was the one who was chosen" must rush through their minds shortly after finding out about their new task. Unfortunately, there are two unintended consequences of this belief that tend to plague organizations for months and years after the news.

To understand the first unintended consequence, we should look to how the belief is formed. In most situations, it goes like this. "The company is in a mess. It needs someone to take it out of the mess. The person chosen will have to be the best at making decisions. I have been chosen. Therefore, I must be the best." There is a sense of logic in this thinking, but the logic may be flawed. First, being the "best" by definition means that there is no one who can make decisions better. This understanding is almost always based on the assumption that "everyone" has been interviewed or thought of for the position. This is rarely the case. The pool of choices is usually culled from a relatively short list of potential managers. Therefore the logical track of belief should be, "I am the best of those considered." Fine. Except that being the best of those considered can have little relevance to meeting the needs of an organization in trouble.

Another unintended consequence of the belief in the "rightness" of decisions is that if one is the "best" at making decisions, and that belief has been reinforced by being given the position of decision maker, why would the manager be willing to be open to learning more? After all, being the best normally rides hand in hand with knowing everything that needs to be known, and if one knows everything that needs to be known about making effective decisions, why would one be willing to be open to learning more? The implications of this can be devastating to an organization and its future. If an organization is run by someone who is not willing to learn more, it will be doomed to be the victim of the same responses, reactions, and techniques that "worked" in a previous situation or organization. Unfortunately, what has worked in the past is not guaranteed to work in a new situation, in a new environment, at a new time.

Decision making is not akin to mathematics where it is possible to prove an answer to a problem. It is possible to prove that $2 + 2$ will always equal 4. It is possible to prove Pythagoras' theorem. But making decisions in organizations is very situational, and the response to a problem in one instance may not work in the next instance. The primary reason for this is that making decisions in organizations affects people, and different people react differently in different situations. In organizational decision making, there is no right answer. There are answers to problems that are better than others, answers that may result in more effective solutions, answers that can yield better results in performance, but there are no right answers.

This chapter deals with an organization that was being driven by someone who believed that he was the "chosen one," the one who was picked to make the decisions because he was always right. And it was this belief in his own infallibility that resulted in increasing levels of lowered effectiveness over time.

ClassCo

ClassCo is one of the oldest organizations used in the development of this book. It has a history that spans almost 100 years, and like many other case studies, had over a period of time established a strong record and reputation for being able to deliver what it promised to its customers. But as in many other cases, this reputation faltered over time and new leadership was brought in to rectify the problem.

In the case of ClassCo, the senior leadership role had gone from a high sense of stability (only five CEOs in more than 70 years) to one of a seemingly revolving door, with four CEOs in the most recent eight-year period. This perception of a revolving door ceased however when the most recent CEO was hired. Initially retained as an interim to replace the previous CEO (who had been dismissed for relative inability to act out responsibilities of office), he came into the organization with a credo about which he was very explicit – the organization was in a mess and he was there to clean it up. His job was not about making friends, it was about "fixing" the mess, and he was the person to do it. Although this message might have been extremely accurate, it sent chills throughout the organization.

The new CEO did go about fixing things, and after the initial interim assignment ended, he was given a contract as "permanent" CEO by the board of directors. This contract has been renewed several times since then, and at the time of writing he is still the head of the organization. What is fascinating about this story is that, although the CEO was visibly closed to new ideas – i.e. "you will do it my way or you can leave" – he was also cognizant that in order to accomplish what he wanted and needed to accomplish, he would have to increase the internal capacity of the organization to learn to become more effective. This awareness helped to create an internal group that focussed their efforts on better understanding of some of the organizational dynamics at play. Through the utilization of systems thinking, the group began to inquire internally as to some of the "stories" that were abounding about the behaviors of the senior management team. In this work, the group were able to identify many of the variables that were impacting the organizational climate, something that they had experienced spiraling downward over the past several years. The variables that stood out included:

- leadership actions
- leadership learning
- organizational climate
- trust
- fear

- level of communications
- level of belief that the organization would ever be able to change.

With these variables, the group began to reconstruct some of the dynamics at play in the organization (*see* Fig 7.1). After a relatively long period of time – the group met once a week over lunch – they were able to develop a set of causal loop diagrams that they felt represented the structure that was driving the organizational culture behaviors. The loops were done on two levels: the organizational-wide level (loop R1) and the personal level (loop R2). The story told by loop R1 made sense to the group. As the organizational climate had been getting worse, there was less sharing and open communication throughout the organization. This led to less potential learning by the senior leadership about what was actually going on in the firm, which in turn led to a decrease in appropriate actions that would have been perceived as positive. This reduced the level of trust and, consequently, sent the climate to even lower levels.

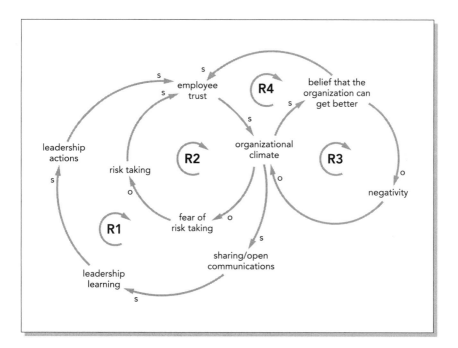

Fig 7.1 The impact of beliefs on culture

On a personal level, loop R2 showed that as the climate declined, there was an increase in the fear associated with risk taking. This led to a decrease in actual risk taking and less trust. This in turn drove the climate even lower. The fact that these two loops were joined at the variable of organizational climate showed the interrelationship between personal actions and organizational outcomes. Loop R2 demonstrated how these dynamics were reinforced by the mental models of the employees. As the climate declined – another connection to the organizational climate – the belief that the organization would or could ever improve again would go down as well. This would lead to higher levels of negativity and further reinforcement of an already declining organizational climate. The group believed that these loops identified the structure that was driving the behaviors that were quite visible within the firm, and then pondered what to do with this knowledge.

After several conversations that seemed to revolve around the question of "so what do we do now?" the group decided to show the structure to the CEO. The hope was that if the CEO could "see" what was impacting the organizational climate, perhaps he would do something about it – something other than constantly berating people for the continued downward slide in climate. The CEO was told that the loops represented structure – they were not meant to say that things were bad or good, simply that this was the structure that was driving the organizational behaviors that no one seemed to like. Just as the loops identified what was happening in the organization, they would also be a way to determine where an appropriate intervention point was to change the "bad news" into "good news." After all, structure does not know any direction, it is simply structure, and can work in either good or bad directions. The group, and the CEO, simply wanted the dynamics to go from a vicious cycle (which it represented at the time) to a virtuous cycle.

> ● By focussing efforts on leadership actions, the group reasoned that, as the actions of the leaders became better, the belief that the behaviors were actually able to get better would be realized.

The learning group identified two areas (variables) that they believed would help reverse the decline in the organizational climate. These two variables were indirectly linked, as were all the variables in the structure, but the group sensed that these two variables would provide the highest leverage for changing the outcomes that were being driven by the structure. The variables were "leadership actions" and "belief that the culture can improve." By focussing efforts on leadership actions, the group reasoned that, as the actions of the leaders became better, the belief that the behaviors were actually able to get better would be realized. Conversely, if the population believed that the organization could actually ever change, the actions of the senior leaders would improve. It was a sort of self-fulfilling prophecy concept – if we can believe that it can get better, it will have the chance to get better, and when that happens, our belief that it can will be reinforced.

This was not easy work. The development of the loops took more than a year of long, hard conversations about the organization, about senior management, and about the mental models of the people who had worked in the organization and seen all the changes over time. But the effort did pay off: through the utilization of the structural diagram, the climate did improve, with a shift in climate from 1.8 on a 5-point Likert scale to 3.5 over a two-year period.

It was at this point in time that the organization began to implement a new enterprise resource planning (ERP) system to replace the "home-built" central computing system. This was to prove to be a good test of how far the organization had come in the past few years regarding internal learning and focus on improving the organizational climate.

Even though most people believed that the organization needed a system that had more power, would be more flexible and responsive, and easier to use, it became apparent quite quickly that this process would not be an easy one. The first problem arose during the vendor selection process. Although the winning vendor was part of a formal proposal and selection process, there were concerns about how the decision had been made to award the contract.

"The vendor's people who made the presentation told us everything we wanted to hear. It was a real sales job."

"I think that someone was under the gun to buy or look for a piece of software and maybe we went a little bit too fast because we were under that gun."

"We never really took a close look in detail to see if it was able to do what we needed in terms of all the parts we needed."

"I was never under the impression when we bought it that we were to be responsible for implementing it, at least not to the level that we have had to do."

"Part of the decision was based, I think, on the fact that we wanted to go on Oracle, because we already were an Oracle database shop, and (the winning vendor's) product was supposed to be on Oracle within a year or so. Their product

was supposed to be out at the end of 1997 or early 1998, and then we would migrate over. Well, neither of those things happened and the Oracle product is not out yet. Maybe in 1999."

"In the presentations, (the winning vendor) showed us these wonderful screens that looked fancy and neat, the whole thing. Even though we knew it was not a true relational database, they promised us that it would be by the time they brought it up. But they didn't deliver on that promise."

Ensuring that needs and expectations are explicit is a key element of any initiative. Ensuring that those needs and expectations can be met is critical. The interviews tell a story of mixed signals concerning the acquisition of the computer solution for the organization. Beliefs that the process was rushed, beliefs that the vendor was the "predetermined" vendor of choice, or beliefs that the acquisition included provisions that it didn't include all contributed to the mixed signals about the process of selection.

How can one avoid this situation in the future? The answer is to make everything visible and explicit. The organization has a long history, and part of that history is a well-established mechanism for turning rumor into reality. The best way to mitigate this potential when conducting future initiatives is to make everything visible and explicit. In a large, complex organization, this is not easy. But the very belief that the organization has more going on than meets the eye, and that it is too complex, complicates the ability to avoid these complications.

"The day the software is installed, basically, it's there and ready to be used. But as we know, there's quite a bit of work that has to be done to get the client running. Implementation is getting people trained, familiar with the new systems, data converted from existing systems to new systems, procedure manuals written on how to use the new system, and then more and more training. A lot of it has to do with cultural change."

"The one thing that almost everybody who implements a system underestimates is the ramp-up time for the technical staff to learn new ways of doing things, regardless of what their previous systems were."

"We made a lot of decisions in too short a time without investigating the manpower needed to implement the decision."

"We were told that our server capacity would be fine for all of this, and it hasn't been."

"The implementation is going much slower that I would have expected to go."

"Well, it could be going better. We are overscheduled now."

"Not enough warm bodies to do the work, the corporate culture of the organization, and the ability of the organization to accept and adapt to change."

"Not only do we not have enough people on the job, we don't have the right match of people and skills and needs."

"We're playing catch-up because we have somewhat the wrong people. We have old systems programers and analysts from the old system."

"I know that the people on top have been told that we need more resources dedicated to this project, but they don't seem to hear."

"I don't believe that our IT people have been largely competent or have the resources to do this work."

"We are beginning to see a lot of little mistakes that wouldn't have happened if we didn't have the problems of burnout and sagging morale regarding the implementation."

"A lot of time was wasted because we weren't always given the information of what needed to be done to implement it right."

"A real sincere buy-in throughout the organization from the beginning would have helped."

"I think that much of the cost of this project has been in lost opportunities."

"A lot of the problems began with unrealistic expectations that weren't able to be met."

"A lot had to do with just up front letting people know that this thing was going to happen."

"More timely testing would have avoided many of the glitches that we have experienced. We were so rushed."

"The workload is not appropriately distributed and that is driven by the fact that the staff is short-handed. Since the project started, IT has lost five people and have replaced only two."

"The vendor's product is not bad, but you need the right resources to support it. If you don't have them, your customers won't be served."

"One reason that so many people have left is probably their creativity was stymied and they knew they couldn't grow within the IT division. They had to leave to grow professionally."

Dealing with change can be hard, especially in a culture that has shown that it doesn't necessarily like change. From the interviews conducted in the process of gathering information on the initiative at ClassCo, it appears that the employees have accepted the new system and are now frustrated by the delays in the implementation process. This frustration will continue until the system is fully operational – and getting this to happen soon might be a problem.

> ● Dealing with change can be hard, especially in a culture that has shown that it doesn't necessarily like change.

When an organization is faced with these types of situations, it is important to realize the impact of focussing on the core competencies of vision, understanding, and systemic thinking on an employee group of a company. In this case study, it was the low level of core competencies that exacerbated the problems facing the organization. By focussing on vision, the organization would have been able to paint a clearer picture of what it was attempting to create with the new system. Although this effort was made several times, the environment of the organization tended to pre-empt the message from being communicated in an effective way and being heard – the core competency of understanding. Employees tended to hear what they believed, and this became a reinforcing spiral so that the news that was floating around the organization became laced with negative connotations as opposed to positive aspects.

As noted in the causal loops shown earlier in this case study, one of the significant variables driving the organization was the "belief that the organization could change." It was a low level of understanding that was causing this variable to spin in a negative direction. The core competency of systemic thinking, and its effective application, would have resulted in a higher level of the overall dynamics of the project and its impact on the organization.

Summary

Is the steering bad or is it just the driver?

What happens when management becomes more important than leadership

ClassCo was in trouble, so it did what so many companies do in that situation: it went out and hired someone to come and "fix" the mess it was in. And fix it it did, but in a way that drove the already sagging organizational culture even deeper. The person who was hired had a reputation of being a turn-around agent. He had "saved" other organizations in the past, but when he came to ClassCo, his experiences were tested to a scale that he had not expected. So he did what many others would do – when you push and the company pushes back, you push harder. He did, and it drove the culture and company effectiveness to a new low.

This is a typical story that exemplifies the difference between management and leadership. The new CEO was a good manager, but struggled with leadership. His style was rough, abrasive, and not focussed on building alignment to meet the challenges the organization was facing. In fact, the level of alignment probably did increase, but the gain in alignment was that he was a problem. To shift the organizational behaviors required the CEO first to understand them, especially the behaviors that were an outcome of the way he treated people.

All this was complicated when ClassCo tried to implement a new technology solution to enable it to better meet its customer needs. These problems could have been mitigated to a great extent through understanding the dynamics at play in the organization, and therefore understanding how those dynamics impact long-term organizational effectiveness.

Key learning

Working to improve the organizational climate in any organization is worth the effort. An organization that has a low climate – a company in which the employees feel disconnected from the management – can result in an inability to effectively implement initiatives, regardless of their relevance and importance to the company's future. It is the structure of an organization that drives its behaviors, and if the behaviors need to be changed, it is the structure that should be addressed – no change in behaviors, no ability to sustain change.

8

I love deadlines, especially the sound they make as they whoosh by

What happens when organizations struggle with change initiatives

One of the greatest problems faced by all organizations that are undergoing dramatic change is ensuring that the employees of a company are willing and able to accommodate the change. In many change efforts it is either an unwillingness or an inability to change that can wreak devastating long-term effects.

Being able to accept change can sometimes be difficult. Although everyone experiences change every day of their lives, it is the realization of this that results in a belief that by resisting change, an employee group can retain the status quo, or at least what they think the status quo is.

When an organization has a long history – in organizational terms this may be only in the 30–40-year range – there can be the belief that "things were just fine in the old days." This is a result of the perceived belief that the "old days" were better because change was an issue. The reality is that organizational change occurred then as well, but for a variety of reasons it was not as apparent. Some of these reasons are due to the speed with which organizations face change today, largely because of the rapid evolution in technology and the increasing number of mergers and acquisitions that employees are experiencing.

This chapter examines one organization that was the target of an acquisition effort. In this case, the employees of the target company experienced a feeling of being "stepchildren," i.e. children of a set of parents that are not treated as well as the natural children.

ScotCo

ScotCo is an organization that has from the start believed in and operated under a strict hierarchy of command and control. Due largely to the organizational structure, both the explicit and implicit messages that come from the senior management reinforce this hierarchy. This has worked well for the organization in the past. But due to the need to be able to adapt to the new technology that appears to be impacting so many organizations, ScotCo has of late been feeling the pressure to improve how it conducts its business. There are few questions or concerns about the fact that it is moving in this direction; the vast majority of concerns revolve around how it is doing it.

The physical structure, i.e. the organizational chart, shows a multi-faceted organization comprised of different business units that all perform the same basic functions – to provide security services to multiple population groups. This has resulted in various dynamics, including the apparent inability of all the business units to buy in to the overall strategy of implementing a computing system that will let all the units "talk" to each other. The rationale is that if they can all communicate better with each other, they can avoid a potential overlap of services, efforts, and the ongoing perception that most of the units are trying to "reinvent the wheel."

"There are eight separate organizations that are buying into this national strategy: We don't all come from the same perspective."

"And one of the problems for implementation strategy is that there is no overall business strategy for the collective organizations. There is no single document you can go to and say 'This is where we are going, therefore we can start addressing some specific issues.' "

An additional dynamic that has impacted the ability of the units to move forward effectively with the technology solution is the variance in unit size. The organization put together a steering committee with representatives of each of the business units to move the implementation forward, but the dynamics of the committee, due to the variance in sizes, appears to have aggravated the situation.

"We have had problems in the past, because we are a big unit, a big unit and six small units. There is a review of the structure of the business units going on … there is a real critical mess with politics … it's a political mess we are trying to reconcile."

"… it's an amorphous, political mess … I think it's the structure of the units and bureaucracy and politics, I come back to the idea that committee needs authority. I have no idea who makes decisions. (A committe member) is a good chairman, but there is no one kicking arse."

The real and perceived power that the business unit leaders had was on the minds of the people involved in the technology project, so much so that it appeared there was a relatively pervasive mental model that the level of power that a business unit leader had was a contributing factor to many of the problems the project was experiencing.

"How much longer can the heads of the business units think they will continue to be an island …? How long before someone says we will have to be joined up with the rest of the world?"

"Business unit leaders tend to be pretty autocratic animals. They are quite powerful individuals and they are very, very proud of the way in which they have worked in the past."

"So how autonomous a business unit leader is is part of the issue."

Not only was the issue of control impacting the committee, the issue of individual business unit agendas and the level of shared collaborative efforts was spinning about as well.

"It reflects a convention in the organizational culture not to collaborate, not to work together. Some things have worked very well, for example the formation of the customer response unit. This one (the technology implementation committee) has followed the same spirit, but it is far more complicated, it needs a far more structured approach."

"Because certainly the bigger business units have more resources and they have been able to be the lead units for this and the lead units for that and nothing has come out of it … I suspect that this is an opportunity for them to get their hands on the money."

"There is a fear that (a big business unit) is leading the strategy."

"Most members are wearing their corporate hats in the meetings, but will protect their own force first."

"Yes … what's the point of me objecting to it, I'll be gone by the time it is delivered."

"The role of the central IT team is unclear."

"I never even knew that there were consultants engaged on this project, and I'm the chairman of (one of the business units). That shows you the communication problems. Nobody communicated it to me. It was in the minutes that they were going to get consultants, but the dates and everything only came yesterday."

"I think that the units don't pass along information well because of the reporting structure within the units."

"There isn't a co-ordinated message – there could be eight different messages going back to the units."

"As far as the units are concerned this is ground-breaking stuff on the technical front, so we've got to accept that there is a learning curve and people will trip up, but I'm not sure we were expecting it to be as bad as it is."

"It isn't really as effective as I hoped it would be."

"There was an expectation that the forces would do more than they have so far."

"I think that there is a mismatch between some of the perceptions of what we actually do and what is in our job descriptions."

"The bottleneck is actually the whole change-readiness issue. We aren't ready."

"One serious gap has been the ability to project manage it and keep the deadlines."

"Decisions are not made during the meetings because the members do not understand the strategy."

When a group of employees respond with words like this, there is a strong indication that the level of understanding is extremely limited. And when this occurs in an organizational structure, especially one that is quite hierarchical in nature as is ScotCo, the perception of "not knowing" quickly changes to one of high perceived complexity. This is due to the lack of information leading to "guessing" what is going on, or believing certain things are going on that, in reality, may not be happening at all. This was the case at ScotCo. This increase in perceived complexity led to a decrease in the willingness to have honest and open communication (*see* Fig 8.1). This was due to a concern about "not knowing," and consequently "not sure" what to say to who. This shift in behaviors was not conducive to an open organizational climate, especially at a time of relatively high organizational change.

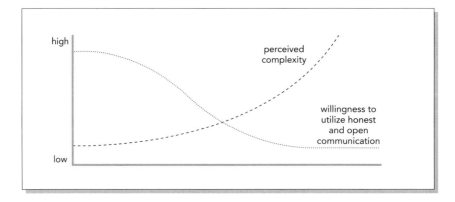

Fig 8.1 Relationship over time between communication and perceived complexity

"People are being asked to make decisions on something they do not understand."

"One major problem is that the units do not really understand the benefit of the project."

"I'm not sure what is right and what is wrong. Should the IT team be going in there and helping out or is it a case that it is up to the units? But whatever the view is, there is not common understanding about this."

"It's a good idea, but it lacks direction, it does not have a day-to-day manager sitting above it."

"And so there is a lot of good will, a lot of agreement on what needs to be done, but there doesn't seem to be a strong carry forward."

"My thought is that everyone is signed up to it, but not able to do that much about it."

"Some people still don't have the message as to what we are trying to do and what the strategy is about."

"There is nothing to show for the work they are doing. There is generally quite low motivation for the job."

"The entire concept needs a bit more direction."

"Well I think there has been some doubt, not in my mind but in the minds of the general community, about where that committee fits in. Do persons on that committee come with delegated responsibility to make executive decisions? It's bureaucratic, it's inept, it's all talk and no action. Who knows what the central team does? I don't. Who knows what they spend the money on? They continue to work, but what are they producing? Are they the right kinds of people? Would the investment be better spent on a more active, recognized, project-type approach? We don't really have a project. If you look for a project, you'd be hard pushed to find one. We're trying to develop a personnel system. You might challenge why we're doing it this way. A lot rests on an all-singing, all-dancing computer system, but do we need that?"

The repeated comments of the team members on the ScotCo project alluded to the need for a concerted effort to increase the visibility of the vision for the project. This might include a view of what it would be like to work in the organization upon the completion of the project, what the benefits of the project were, and how the work environment would improve upon completion. Additionally, it would be highly beneficial to put forth an effort to enhance the level of understanding within the organization, i.e. training the employees to listen empathically and to communicate more effectively than they had been doing. By using systemic thinking, by making the case for the project using the concepts and methods most commonly associated with systems thinking, the project team would be better able to see the dynamics impacting the organization, both at the present time and after the implementation of the computer system. By using systemic thinking, they could

> ● It would be highly beneficial to put forth an effort to enhance the level of understanding within the organization.

better see that the new computer system was not the "answer." It is just a tool, but a tool that should help to increase the quality of their work over time.

Summary

I love deadlines, especially the sound they make as they whoosh by

What happens when organizations struggle with change initiatives

ScotCo is interesting. It is a large organization that serves a geographically diverse customer population group with business units of various sizes and, consequently, various levels of resources, even though all the business units are expected to deliver the same service and the same service level. Business unit managers were in a quandary – how could they possibly deliver the same services and same service level with vast differences in resources? This was complicated by a dynamic that is represented by the saying "the rich get richer, and the poor get poorer." This growing gap between haves and have-nots was causing massive problems for senior management, and the way they decided to deal with the gap was not based on a thorough under-standing of the dynamics at play in the organization. Increasing the ability of the business unit leaders to share collective resources through building a shared vision, shared understanding and shared ability to think systemi-cally would have mitigated many of the problems.

Key learning

When an organization is geographically diverse, efforts to build a collective culture can be difficult, but are extremely important. Geographic diversity in today's world does not automatically result in fractionalized efforts, and, conse-quently, fractionalized results. Building a shared culture, with shared values and shared understanding of vision and mission, always brings a high return on investment.

9

I can smell the smoke but I can't see the fire

What happens when we lose sight of the real goal

Reorganization has become the fix-all for organizations in today's world. In previous times, when an organization needed to grow, it tended to accomplish this through applied efforts to gain market share through strategy; when an organization needed to reduce expenses, it tended to accomplish this by examining how it spent it money. But in today's world, growth strategies have been replaced by acquisitions and cost reductions have been replaced by massive reductions in the areas that are most visible – labor and capital expenditures. This is the typical firefighting approach.

Organizations today are filled with people who wish to be known as effective firefighters – those who, when faced with a problem (an organizational fire), are known to be able to "put it out." This has set up a system in which the firefighters appear to be valued far more than others and has been seen in organizations of all types in the business media for some time. Firefighting has become the way to become more effective, more recognized, and more rewarded. But continually firefighting and reorganizing in an organization is not much different than a doctor performing radical surgery on someone who is suffering from a pain but chooses not to change his or her behavior.

Here is a typical scenario faced by parents. Your daughter has trouble riding her bicycle and keeps falling down. Every time this happens, she comes into the house with bloody knees and elbows. The question becomes, is it better to help her learn how to balance while attempting to ride the bike, or is it simply easier to sell the bike and amputate the legs and arms that keep getting skinned on the street? Apparently, according to the way in which firefighters have been managing organizations, it is better to opt for the radical surgery. After all, it will stop the problem of falling off the bike. What is missed here, however, is that the child will never be able to realize her potential for riding.

This is what is happening day after day in organizations now. Instead of investing in the long-term future of an organization by creating an environment in which it can realize its potential, when it is facing problems senior management tend to take the path of reorganization. In many cases this means massive lay-offs, reduction in assets, and shifts in capacity building. Is this so different from any other radical surgery?

The front page of the *Financial Times* on Thursday 10 June, 2000 told the story. Procter & Gamble (P&G), the world's biggest consumer company, was about to undertake yet another major restructuring effort. The plan as announced called for the organization to "cut 15,000 jobs at a cost of $1.9 billion" over a five-year period. The CEO stated that the firm "had not invented a new category of products since 1982" and that the aim was "to halve the time it took to bring new products to the market."

On the surface, this made sense. Procter & Gamble had focussed on bringing some of the existing products into new and emerging markets since the 1980s and that focus had "come at the expense of innovation." Due to this strategy, P&G has missed many sales targets and was far behind its target of doubling its sales by 2006. By cutting jobs and expenses, the firm believed it could renew itself to regain its growth and position in the marketplace. That is the "on-the-surface view."

Viewing the statements in the *FT* systemically, the relationships of actions tell us that as P&G reduces the number of jobs, it will become more flexible, enabling it to react more effectively (*see* Fig 9.1). This will stimulate its growth, enabling it to gain market position. Few would dispute this as a sound strategy. But when organizations make such pronouncements, it is always interesting to look at some of the potential unintended consequences to stated actions and strategies. By looking at some of the unintended consequences of this strategy, we might gain insights into the potential for its success over time.

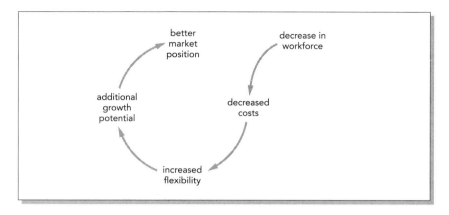

Fig 9.1 The effect of reducing the number of jobs

As the number of jobs decreases, besides becoming more flexible in the market there is an increase in the fear of losing one's job. This will lead to a decrease in the level of personal commitment to the organization, i.e. "if there is the potential that I might lose my job, then why should I be committed to the organization and its strategy?" A possible assumption might be that as this commitment decreases, the potential for innovation will decrease, thus reducing the potential for growth in the marketplace. This will lead to more restructuring efforts, again reducing jobs. Another concern will be the impact of stress on those remaining in the organization. As the number of employees is reduced, the workload on those remaining will grow, increasing the potential for stress regarding how to "get all the work done," and "will it be my turn to go next?" Both of these will serve to increase stress and decrease morale and commitment. This dynamic – a morale/commitment loop – is known as a vicious cycle – it will continue unless the structure that is driving these "behaviors" is changed (*see* Fig 9.2).

Another unintended consequence could be the loss of organizational memory (*see* Fig 9.3). When organizations restructure through job cutbacks, one of the potential outcomes is the loss of key people who have a long history with the organization. This can be due to the way used most often to

> ● As the number of jobs decreases, besides becoming more flexible in the market there is an increase in the fear of losing one's job.

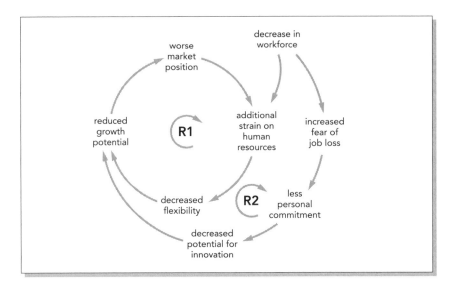

Fig 9.2 The effect on personal commitment

conduct cutbacks – buy out employees who are near to retirement age. Again, on the surface this methodology of cutting back seems sound – lay off those who are the easiest to let go without resorting to major lay-offs in the areas of production. But the oldest employees are usually the ones who have been with the organization the longest, and it is this population group which has the highest level of organizational memory. Organizational memory is the glue that holds the organization together. It is the organizational memory that is the basis for the culture of the organization – the stories, the values, the implicit policies and procedures, and the foundation for who and what the collective organization is.

> ● Organizational memory is the glue that holds the organization together.

As the organizational memory decreases, the potential to lose the implicit policies and procedures (the way things really get done in an organization, not the stated policies and procedures) increases. This will decrease the potential for growth over time. Once again, this demonstrates a vicious cycle that will continue to push the organization into more restructuring over time.

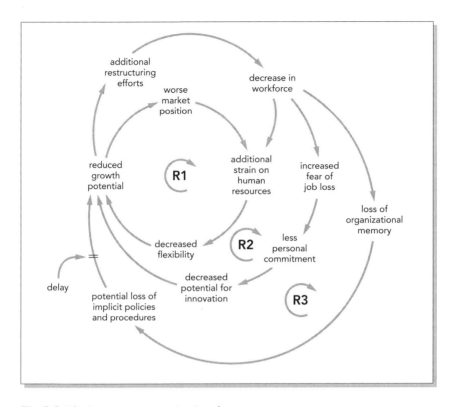

Fig 9.3 The impact on organizational memory

Another, and perhaps the most vicious, dynamic that might occur from this new round of restructuring is a dynamic known as "gaming the system." Gaming the system refers to what happens in an organizational culture when plans are put into place that result in changes in the way that things get done in the organization.

There are several ways in which gaming the system may begin to occur in this type of situation, including reward structure gaming, alignment mismatch gaming, and inadequate infrastructure gaming.

When carrying out a typical restructuring policy, one of the prime motivators is the reward structure. In most cases, that can equate to organizational managers being rewarded financially for managing to achieve new organizational goals while in a restructured environment. One of the problems with this type of environment is that as a result of the restructuring policy that culminated in fewer employees, it is more difficult to achieve increased production goals, and increased production goals are what is needed to ensure organizational success. By offering rewards to managers who can successfully manage in the new environment, the tendency can be for the managers to game the system to effectively show positive results. This can manifest itself in accelerated billings, overly optimistic production numbers, and other areas of "creative accounting."

Alignment mismatch gaming can occur when the goals of one manager in the new organization do not match the goals of another manager. This can result in managers becoming accidental adversaries of other managers in the overall organization. The organizational operating model says that each manager works his or her area to maximize the return. This in turn increases the potential of overall organizational success (*see* Fig 9.4).

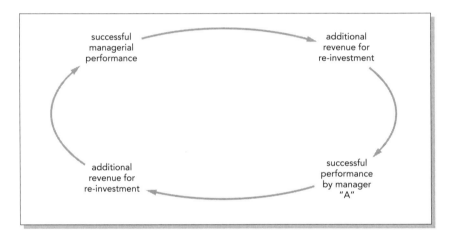

Fig 9.4 Desired collaborative relationship

However, when there is a mismatch in alignment of goals, managers do what they believe they need to do to ensure success for their department or division, sometimes negatively impacting the potential of another department or division. This shifts the overall dynamic, causing the overall organizational potential to decrease.

As can be seen in Fig 9.5, the dynamic structure changes from "good news" to "bad news" when managers have an alignment mismatch in goals. As each manager struggles to meet the new standards of performance that traditionally accompany a restructuring effort, their individual efforts can be detrimental to the efforts of other managers.

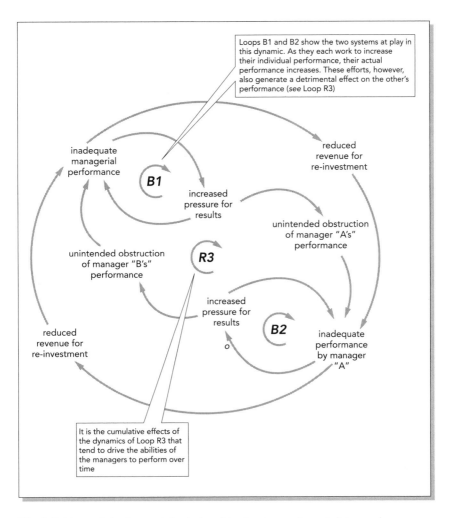

Fig 9.5 Potential adversarial relationship due to a mis-match in goals

Restructuring can often result in an inadequate infrastructure – the infrastructure is unable to cope with the changes in the organizational structure brought about by the restructuring effort. This is usually due to the inability of the organization to get everything "ready" for the restructuring prior to its commencement. When this happens, managers believe they are forced into "flexing" the policies and procedures to meet the new organizational goals. This can result in long-term systemic problems that will manifest themselves in reduced organizational potential over time.

Organizational restructuring is not new, and in many cases has resulted in increased viability for many organizations. Organizations that have restructured have seen increased levels of stock price and demand for products. However, there are many unintended consequences to reorganizational efforts. The short-term gains are very visible and positive in the view of investors. The long-term impacts are usually negative and can result in additional restructuring efforts – as seen in the case of Procter & Gamble.

Can organizations avoid the potential unintended consequences of restructuring? Only through looking systemically at the dynamics of the organization before, during, and after the restructuring effort.

Summary

I can smell the smoke but I can't see the fire

What happens when we lose sight of the real goal

Reorganization seems to be one of the methods of choice to increase organizational effectiveness, and consequently profits and share price. But reorganization as an implicit strategy can lead to short-term reactive thinking. Conversely, reorganization is in many cases a result of short-term reactive thinking as well. It is the current "quick fix" for many of the ills from which companies are suffering, and although in many cases it is probably appropriate, it is generally a short-term fix, not a sustainable solution. In every case I have seen, a more fundamental solution can be found by focussing efforts on increasing organizational effectiveness. The reason is that reorganization deals only with visible events such as costs and profits. By reorganizing, costs are reduced and profits increase. But the fundamental problems that put the company in a situation where these events were out of balance are never addressed. By focussing on sustainable solutions, a company can not only increase effectiveness, it can, over time, see a shift in expenses and profits as an outcome.

The main problem is that senior managers in most companies are rewarded for fixing and reacting quickly to problems, i.e. organizational fires. We need to train our managers at all levels to focus on building environments in which we do not have the fires that cause reactive thinking – no fires, no need to fight fires. Sustainable thinking will outweigh short-term reactive thinking every time. Too bad we don't have reward systems for managers that drive those behaviors.

Key learning

When contemplating a restructuring initiative, it is important to realize the impact it will have on the employees. It is critical to be focussed on dealing with the dynamics that will surface, to be open and honest with employees about the purpose of the initiative and the rationale behind it, and to be willing to explore other options. Short-term thinking breeds short-term results that are not sustainable over time. And by then, the anticipated benefits of the restructuring may result in behaviors that use restructuring to "fix" any problem that arises. Focus on the long-term issues that revolve around sustainability if you want your organization to endure.

10

Where is Picasso when we need him?

What happens when we can't understand the big picture

There has been much written about mental models. For many in the general business population, the first awareness of mental models came in *The Fifth Discipline* by Peter Senge, in which he defines mental models as the "images, assumptions, and stories which we carry in our minds of ourselves, other people, institutions, and every aspect of the world." This chapter is not presented to define mental models further, but instead to explore how the mental models of a group of employees can and have impacted the ability of the organization to realize its potential.

Several years ago, at the commencement of Amherst College, the famous jazz trumpeter Wynton Marsalis told a story. In this story, he recalled how, as a struggling young musician, he and one of his mentors went to the Metropolitan Museum of Modern Art in New York. While walking among the many exhibits, they came upon an exhibition of paintings by Pablo Picasso. Marsalis stopped at one rather spectacular painting and wondered aloud to his mentor, "What is with that Picasso? He is so famous, his pictures sell for millions of dollars, everyone recognizes him as one of the world's greatest painters, and yet some of his pictures just don't make any sense. What is with that Picasso?"

His mentor looked at the painting, then turned to Marsalis and asked him to look at him. "Wynton," he said, "I want you to look straight at my face and describe what you see." Marsalis wasn't sure what this was all about, but respectful of the wisdom of his mentor, he began to describe what he saw. "Well, you have two eyes, one on each side of your nose, just where they are supposed to be. Your nose is in the middle of your face, just where it is supposed to be. I can see parts of both of your ears, one on each side of your head, just where they are supposed to be. And your mouth is located just below your nose, just where it is supposed to be." The mentor then turned his head and repeated the question.

'Well, I can see your right eye, the right side of your nose, your right ear and that's about all," Marsalis replied, adding that they were "all where they were supposed to be." The mentor then turned again, this time letting his student see the other side of his head, and repeated the question once more. Marsalis, not sure what this exercise was meant to accomplish, but still trusting his mentor, gave his description. "Now I can see your left eye, the left side of your nose, your left ear, and they are all where they are supposed to be." Turning once more, the mentor, facing away from Marsalis, said, "Wynton, describe to me what you see." Marsalis proceeded to explain that all he could see was the back of his mentor's head – just hair and the edges of both ears, but that they were located where they should be.

The mentor turned to face the student and, smiling slightly, said that what Wynton had described was probably the same thing that Picasso would have described had he been there. "Then why do his paintings all look like they do?" Marsalis asked. The mentor suggested that perhaps Picasso was simply painting what he saw, and that what he saw were all the dimensions of someone's head at the same time. "If you could see all the various dimensions of my head at the same time, maybe you would paint the picture the same way."

When a large number of company employees see things differently, it follows that the various constituency groups of that population will potentially take different routes to achieve organizational-wide goals. Being able to "see" and understand all the various dimensions of an organization can result in higher levels of alignment regarding not only what to do but how to do it. Being able to see and understand all the various dimensions of an organization can and usually does increase the chances of an organization realizing its potential. Instead of focussing organizational efforts on closing the gap in alignment in how we see an organization, perhaps it might be more effective to focus efforts on why we all see it differently.

At a time when organizations are faced with more apparent complexity and an increasing need to become effective, having alignment in organizational operating models becomes a crucial element for long-term, sustainable success. Alignment is a function of understanding, i.e. if I do not understand what is expected of me, it is difficult to believe that I will be able to act in congruence with those expectations. It therefore follows that in order to ensure that we can act in congruence with those expectations, we must be able to see and understand the world in which we work. By understanding the beliefs and perceptions of various population groups within a large organization, we can better understand why the organization achieves the outcomes it does, as well as illuminating some of the potential limits to effectiveness.

To explore the impact of collective perceptions and beliefs, a research project began, and the researcher focussed on the various perceptions and beliefs about the operating model of a large international service provider. Through the utilization of the concepts and theories of systems thinking, the researcher was able to illuminate multiple views of cross-sectional population groups from within the organization. These views are presented here in the form of causal loop diagrams – models that graphically demonstrate the interrelationships between causes and effects that are evident to the people who constructed them (*see* Figs 10.13–10.15 later).

GlobalCo

Overview of the organization

GlobalCo is a large, multinational organization service provider that demonstrated an exceptional growth rate during the 1990s. From a headcount of 60 in 1995 to approximately 600 in 1999, and a revenue increase of 411 percent in the same period, the organization has been able to consistently set high growth goals for itself and has plans to continue this growth pattern. Several dynamics have been contributing factors to this growth. In the early 1990s, the size of the organization was conducive to a high level of alignment in the goals and strategies of the company, i.e. a smaller organization made it easier to effectively communicate the overall operating model and the accompanying strategies for growth. But as the headcount began to increase, the perceived complexity of the organization

> ● When there was a smaller number of employees, it was easier for management to ensure that initiatives were in alignment with each other.

grew as well. This made it more difficult to ensure that all the newly hired employees would be able to "see" and understand the operating model. With a headcount that has increased ten-fold in just four years, this level of complexity, either real or perceived, has increased dramatically.

Another dynamic during the growth pattern that has become visible is the level of fragmentation of efforts. When there was a smaller number of employees, it was easier for management to ensure that initiatives were in alignment with each other. This kept the level of potential fragmentation – i.e. employees going off in different directions with individually inspired initiatives – to a minimum. But as the organization has grown, the level of alignment has decreased and the level of potential fragmentation has increased. This has been demonstrated in employees' views of the organizational operating model. It is important to realize that although these dynamics have surfaced, this does not mean that the organization is not successful – it only means that the organization may not be realizing its potential due to the levels of alignment and potential fragmentation.

The process

To see better the varying degrees of alignment and potential fragmentation, a series of facilitated sessions was held over a period of six months with cross-sectional employee groups. These groups were selected for their diversity in the organizational hierarchical structure, and were all facilitated by the same person to ensure the ability to compare the resultant views. The views that were developed by the groups are shown as causal loop diagram maps (Figs 10.1 and 10.2).

Each of the views developed in the facilitated sessions was in response to the question, "What are the dynamics of the GlobalCo operating model?" Each group spent approximately 20 minutes in the development of their view, and, most importantly, each group was able to use the semantics that they felt most clearly represented what they meant in their model. After completion of the models, the outputs were "reconstructed" utilizing computer software to enable the researcher to more clearly examine the perceived dynamics at play from each group.

An initial comparison of the models yields two interesting findings. First, all the models except one reflect the same basic picture – a view from

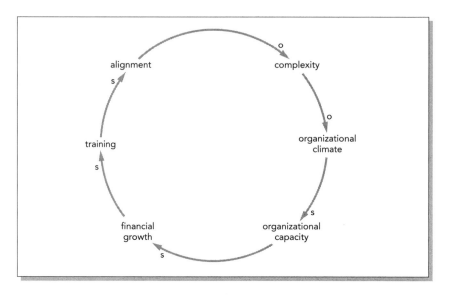

Fig 10.1 Impact of alignment on complexity

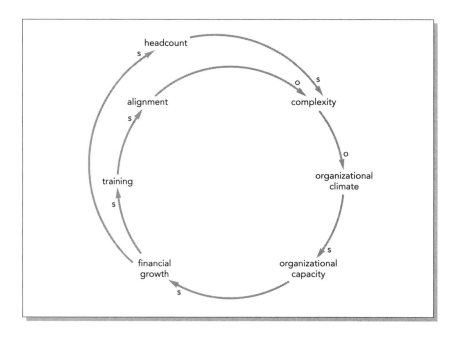

Fig 10.2 The conflict of growth becoming its own limit

the "front lines" of the organization. The single picture that looks different is model C (*see* Fig 10.5). This model represents the view of a senior management official of GlobalCo, whereas the balance of the models represent views of other organizational levels. This variance in perspective is not unusual. In most organizations, senior management tends to operate from a "30,000 feet" view, whereas most organizational employees view the organization from about "3 feet." This variance in perspective can result in causal loop model representations that reflect those views.

A second finding from the model comparison is that all the loops, although representing the same picture, look different. This difference is manifested in the utilization of semantics. Some views use words such as morale, employee satisfaction, and working conditions, all apparently representing the same mental model – a mental model that is supported by the belief that "how we feel about the working environment" has an impact on the organizational dynamics. When faced with the potential that different facilitated groups were using different words to represent virtually the same mental models, it became apparent to the researcher that it was necessary to examine the commonality between the variables used in the models.

A comparison was made to identify common variables, i.e. semantics used to describe an element of the operating model as seen by each group. The variables that were examined related to the dynamics of both alignment and complexity. They included variables that related to headcount, complexity, financial growth, accountability, leadership, training, organizational climate, personal commitment, integration, innovation, organizational capacity, and alignment. When the causal maps were examined, the following variables were identified (the letter refers to which model, followed by the actual descriptive semantic variable). Although these groupings of variables are not meant to be complete, they do give the reader the opportunity to examine some of the mental models that were guiding the thoughts in the participants' minds.

As the reader can see, some of the variables that are related to the listed topic areas are prevalent in many of the models, while some appear in only a few models. Of note are organizational headcount growth-related variables (appearing in 12 models); complexity related variables (appearing in nine models); financial growth-related variables (appearing in 11 models); training-related variables (appearing in ten models); organizational climate-related variables (appearing in 11 models); organizational capacity-related variables (appearing in nine models); and alignment-related variables (appearing in nine models). It is this recurrence of common themes that is of interest when conducting research into why employees behave in the way that they do.

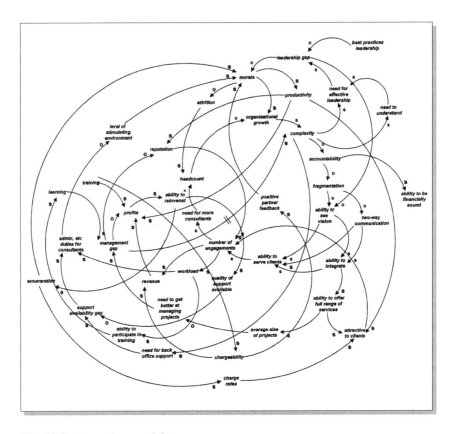

Fig 10.3 Operating model A

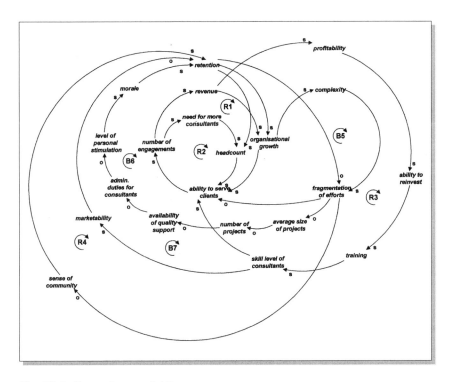

Fig 10.4 Operating model B

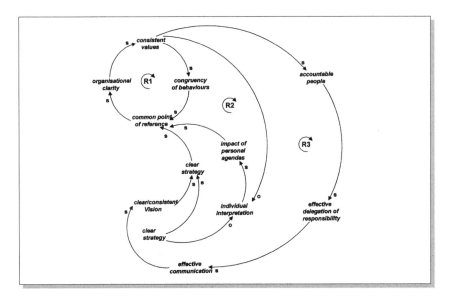

Fig 10.5 Operating model C

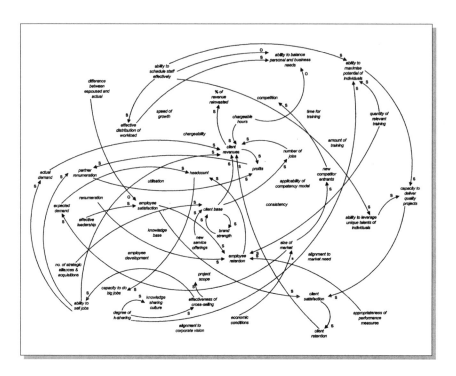

Fig 10.6 Operating model D

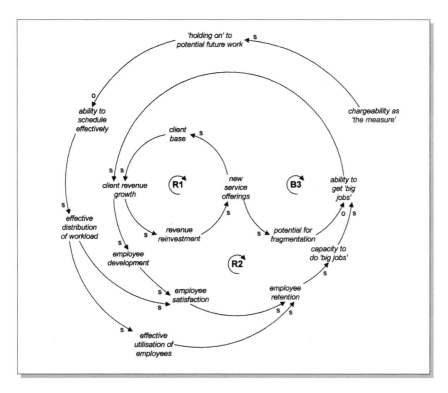

Fig 10.7 Operating model E

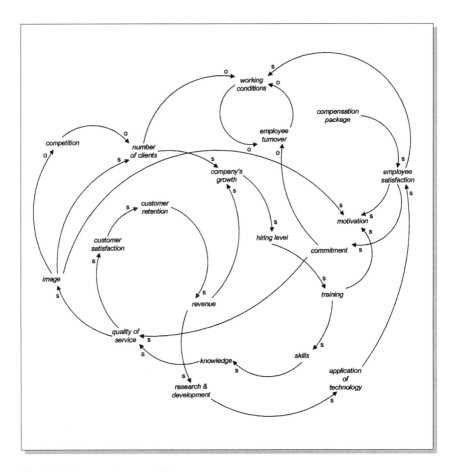

Fig 10.8 Operating model F

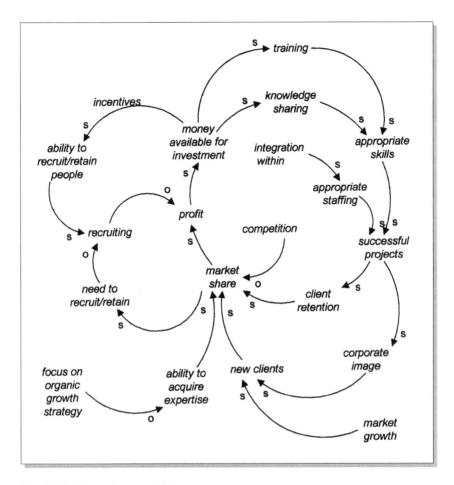

Fig 10.9 Operating model G

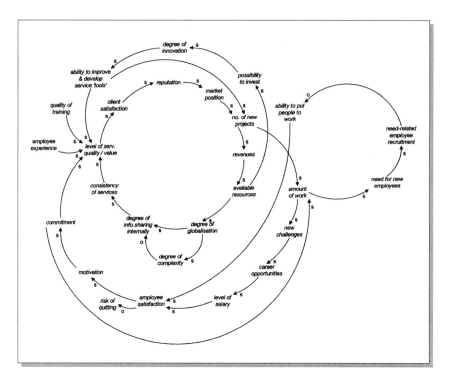

Fig 10.10 Operating model H

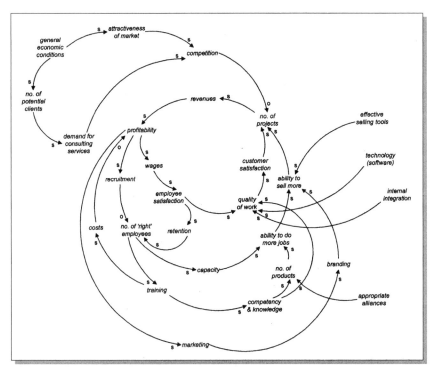

Fig 10.11 Operating model I

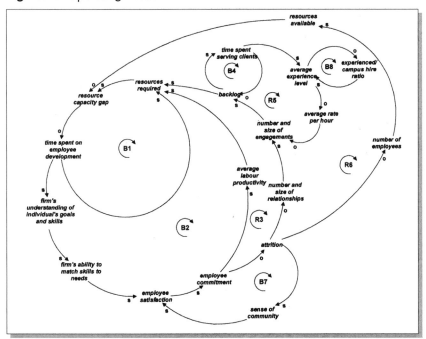

Fig 10.12 Operating model J

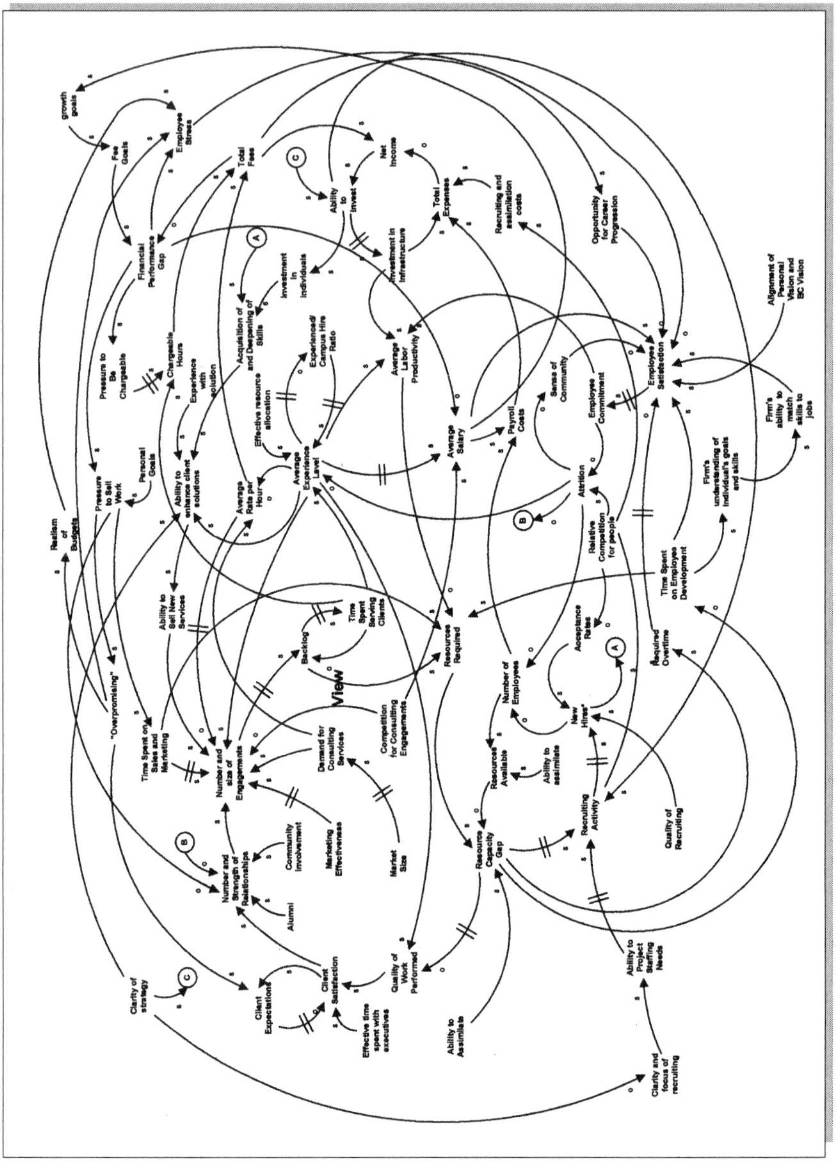

Fig 10.13 Operating model K

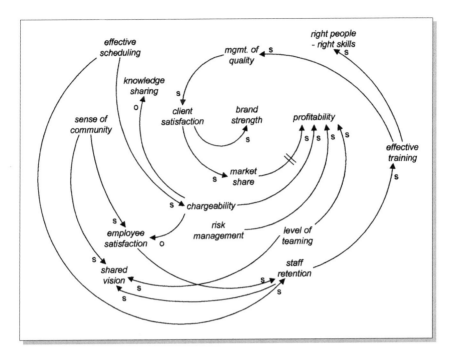

Fig 10.14 Operating model L

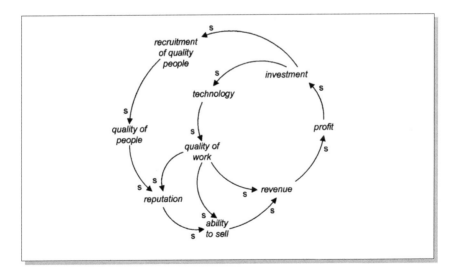

Fig 10.15 Operating model M

Complexity-related variables

A complexity

B complexity

C individual interpretation

D ability to schedule staff effectively

E potential for fragmentation

H consistency of services

J ability to match skills to needs

K ability to match skills to jobs

L effective scheduling

Accountability-related variables

A accountability

C accountable people, effective delegation of responsibility

E effective distribution of workload, holding on to potential work

G focus on organic growth strategy

K overpromising, quality of work performed

L risk management, management of quality

M quality of work

Financial growth-related variables

A revenue, profits, ability to re-invest

B revenue, profitability, ability to re-invest

D revenues, profits, percentage of revenue re-invested

E revenue growth, revenue re-investment

F revenue

G profit, money available for re-investment

H revenues, possibility to invest

I revenues, profitability

K net income, ability to invest

   L profitability

   M revenue, profit, investment

Leadership-related variables

   A management gap, leadership gap, need for effective leadership

   C congruency of behaviors

   D effective leadership

Commitment (personal)-related variables

   F commitment

   J employee commitment

   K employee commitment

Training-related variables

   A training, learning

   B training, skill level

   D quantity of relevant training

   E employee development

   F training, skills

   G training, appropriate skills

   H quality of training

   I training, competency, and knowledge

   K time spent on employee development

   L effective training

Organizational climate-related variables

   A level of stimulating environment, morale

   B level of personal stimulation, morale

   C consistent values

   D employee satisfaction

E   employee satisfaction

F   working conditions

H   employee satisfaction

I   employee satisfaction

J   employee satisfaction

K   employee satisfaction

L   employee satisfaction

Integration-related variables

H   degree of information sharing internally

Innovation-related variables

H   degree of innovation, ability to improve and develop service tools

Alignment-related variables

A   two-way communications, ability to see vision

B   sense of community

C   effective communication, common point of reference, individual inter-
    pretation, clear/consistent vision, clear strategy

D   alignment to corporate vision

G   integration within organization

H   consistency of services

J   sense of community

K   sense of community

L   shared vision

One conclusion that can be drawn from these models is that the recurrence of certain variable semantics might lead one to presume that these are the variables that are most visible in the participants' minds, i.e. these variables are the most common across various population groups within the GlobalCo organization.

If this conclusion is valid, it would be appropriate to "test" out the dynamic relationships of the variables identified. For this we have used the variables of headcount, complexity, financial growth, training, organizational climate, organizational capacity, and alignment. By applying these variables to a set of systems thinking archetypes, we can begin to realize the potential dynamics that will be at play in GlobalCo in the future. A belief of systems thinking is that "structure drives behavior." These variables and their interrelationships represent structure, a structure that revolves around GlobalCo policies and procedures (both implicit and explicit), implicit and explicit organizational goals, and the individual and collective mental models of the employees of GlobalCo.

As can be seen in this structure, as the alignment of the organization increases, the perceived level of complexity decreases. This in turn increases the level of organizational climate, thus increasing the capacity of the organization. This will enable more financial growth, allowing more training and consequently higher levels of alignment. This dynamic represents a high-level view of the GlobalCo growth engine – the dynamic that will allow GlobalCo to continue its growth pattern.

However, as this is a structure, and structures do not determine direction, only dynamics, we can see in Fig 10.2 that as the organization growth continues, more employees are hired. This tends to increase the complexity of the organization, decreasing the climate. This can decrease the overall capacity of the organization, its growth level, its ability to train, and its level of alignment. This dynamic represents the GlobalCo limit to growth. Ironically, the limit to growth of GlobalCo is the same structure that enables its growth.

When examining how a group of employees "sees" its operating model, it is important to realize that all the views may not be the same. In the example of GlobalCo, the views are quite disparate. Some of the causal maps that were developed to demonstrate how the populations "see" the model look quite simple (models C and M) while some appear to be quite chaotic (models A, D, and K).

This signifies an environment in which the population making the causal map is able to see and experience more detail in their perceptions about how the organization works. This is not good news or bad news, only a reflection of how a given population group sees the organization. However, it should also be recognized that the level of complexity of the models demonstrates that there is a variance in the perceptions of the dynamics at play in the organization, and it is this complexity that can severely limit the organization's ability to realize its potential over time. In the case of GlobalCo, this limiting factor is compounded by the identification of the organization's limit to its growth – its own growth pattern over time.

When faced with this level of complexity – the GlobalCo growth engine itself enables the organization's limit to growth – it is important to realize that in most organizations, it is the employees' inability to recognize the dynamics at play that usually inhibits their ability to realize the organization's potential. In the GlobalCo example, the better the organization did, the more it grew. The more it grew, the more complex it became. And eventually, it will see the growth pattern itself become its own limiting factor. This raises several questions for enhancing the strategic initiatives of the GlobalCo organization.

First of these questions is, "What is most important, growth or sustainability?" In the case of GlobalCo, these two issues were interlinked – the senior management believed that to be sustainable, it would need to grow. This, according to the structural model shown in Fig 10.2, is true. The limiting factor of growth will be visible as oscillation – as the limiting factor kicks in, it will limit growth, but as the cycle repeats itself, it will stimulate growth. This would allude to the understanding that the growth pattern of the organization may slow but can be sustained over time.

A second question is, "How can we mitigate the effects of the limit to growth?" Again, we can look to the structural model to help find the answer. By reinforcing the variable of training during the vicious cycle stage of the dynamics, we can reverse the downward spiral of growth. This would require a strong commitment to the belief that training the new employees in the key elements of the GlobalCo organization is critical. In the case of GlobalCo, these training elements include organizational learning, culture, values, their operating model, and other foundational skills.

A third question is, "Can't we simply push past the limiting factor with the sheer momentum of the organization?" This may be a viable option in the short term, but eventually the structural dynamics that are driving organizational behaviors will overtake the growth engine, and over time begin to decrease the growth pattern.

> ● It is important to realize that in most organizations, it is the employees' inability to recognize the dynamics at play that usually inhibits their ability to realize the organization's potential.

A last question might be, "How can we avoid the traditional behavior of cutting training when the going gets tough?" The answer to this question can be found in a one-word answer: commitment. If GlobalCo is truly committed to moving its organization forward through the oscillating cycles that are shown in the structural maps, it must be committed to prioritizing its training program and to focus it on increasing the capacity of the organization to learn both functional skills (the skills it takes to do the individual and collective jobs of the company) and foundational skills (the skills it takes to understand the dynamics and build alignment within the employees). Without a high level of prioritization on training, GlobalCo's ability to continue to grow will be diminished dramatically over time.

Summary

Where is Picasso when we need him?
What happens when we can't understand the big picture

GlobalCo was in a quandary. How could it become more effective? It threw resources at the problem, it communicated with its people, it trained its people. The only thing it forgot to do was to explore how the employees were receiving the resources, the messages, and the training. Most people would agree that several people can look at the same picture and "see" different things. That was what was happening at GlobalCo – everyone was seeing the organization differently. When trying to see how some of the business units viewed the operating model – a common operating model – it became apparent that they all viewed it differently. So it was no wonder that they all had different results.

By looking at the commonalities and differences in how the operating model was viewed, it was possible to determine how best to close the gap. Closing the gap in alignment in how an operating model is viewed is important, but gaining an understanding of how the gap occurred might be more important – if a gap occurred in the first place, it will probably reappear thanks to the structure that was driving the behaviors of the business unit managers.

Key learning

Be aware that for a variety of reasons, employees may have different mental models about how the organization actually works. This "alignment gap" can be devastating to the long-term ability of the organization to realize its potential. Always work to determine what gap is at play in your company, and just as important, why the gap exists. Talk about it. Do something about it. Be willing to explore the gap with your employees. They will be able to provide incredible insights to answer both questions, and will be extremely useful in helping you to close the gap.

11

Not quite as easy as tab A into slot B, but …

Conclusion from the stories

Organizational effectiveness is a complex issue. Based on varied experiences, individuals have developed differing mental models as to what organizational effectiveness even is. To many, it is best exemplified by event-oriented measures, i.e. stock price, return on investment, inventory turns, and profit margins, to mention just a few. To others, indicators of organizational effectiveness include "softer" measures such as the ability to satisfy an organizational mission or purpose.

After conducting research on the issue, I have concluded that organizational effectiveness is a combination of both, and for the purposes of this book will refer to it as the measure of how well an organization can satisfy its mission or purpose over time. The key words here are *over time*. Effectiveness as a measure of how an organization is doing, to be realistic, must include both event-oriented issues – the tangible, easily identifiable measures such as stock price, return on investment, etc. – and those issues that are more structural in nature – how well an organization satisfies its mission or purpose. To ensure that the measures reflect reality, however, means that the measures must be done *over time*.

Measures that are not made over time can result in short-term thinking. Short-term thinking is believed to have resulted in many of the well-known organizational failures that have been so visible in the news over the past few decades (Kotter, 1995). According to data from *Fortune* magazine, "a full one-third of the companies listed in the 1970 Fortune 500 had vanished by 1983." An appropriate question might be, "Why do so many well-known organizations fail?" I believe the answer can be found in their lack of ability to be effective, i.e. satisfy their mission or purpose over time. Almost any organization can produce what we traditionally consider to be excellent results – high profits, high market share, growing stock price, and multiple inventory turns. But the ability of an organization to be able to do this consistently over time appears to be quite elusive. There are many reasons for this.

Event-oriented data, or "hard data," is something that most organizations track quite well. Corporate statements are broken into two sections, the balance sheet and the income statement. These two documents reflect the propensity on the part of organizations to measure hard data. Balance sheets document items such as inventory, cash on hand, investments, and liabilities. Income statements document items such as sales and revenues, and expenses. Nowhere on these documents – both of which reflect the "worth" of an organization – do we see the ability of a group of employees to utilize these resources. Organizational balance sheets do not reflect the value of a sound organizational culture. They do not reflect the impact of employees in sharing a vision of where the organization is going or what its mission or purpose is. And they do not reflect what I believe to be key variables that impact organizational effectiveness. This demonstrates a short-term, myopic view on the part of the stockholders and senior management of our organizations today.

The research I have conducted as part of the development of this book has focussed on issues that have traditionally been thought of as "soft measures" of effectiveness. These include the level and impact of organizational alignment on organizational culture, and the ability to understand organizational mission and purpose. Although not as visible in organizations as "hard" or more traditional measures, it is the non-traditional measures of effectiveness that are foundational in an organization's ability to be sustainable over time.

There are many reasons for organizational inability to be sustainable over time. One of them is the amount of change that an organization undergoes. One of the frustrations heard most often in organizations today is the belief that change seems to be becoming constant. The change being talked about is organizational change, or in today's semantics, corporate reorganization. Reorganization itself has become a service industry, a focus for authors, and so entrenched in our culture that we expect that our organizations will be reorganized over and over again. This usually results in a lowering of organizational effectiveness – the ability of an organization to satisfy its mission. And as the effectiveness of an organization decreases, its ability to be sustainable over time decreases as well.

The implicit intent of most reorganization activities is to help the subject organization become more effective and, therefore, more sustainable over time. However, the evidence of long-term increases in potential sustainability is minimal. This can be due to either the lack of ability to create measures that reflect sustainability as a goal, or the short-term focus of the efforts – either can lead one to the conclusion that our organizations are focussing more and more on what is urgent, not on what is important. What is also becoming apparent is the level of stress among the people affected by the change initiatives. An appropriate question might be, "Why then, if sustainability is important, does it seem that many senior managers are becoming addicted to constant organizational change?"

When all the rhetoric is washed away, the vast majority of change initiatives are reorganization plans. This can be for many reasons – the organization's perceived inability to compete in the marketplace, the perceived level of organizational effectiveness, the organization's ability to obtain the resources it believes it needs to exist, and the organization's perceived ability to plan strategically. In all these situations, the key element is the organization's "perception" of itself.

There is a connective relationship between an employee's perception of themselves and their ability to understand the current reality. It is becoming more evident that employees, including senior management, are busy focussing on initiatives that target current reality issues and not those that will have fundamental impacts on the potential future organizational state, i.e. they are focussed on initiatives that are urgent, and not on those that are important (*see* Fig 11.1). This figure shows the interrelationship between organizational focus and the potential to be sustainable over time. As an organization places its focus on initiatives that are urgent but not important, its ability to be sustainable decreases (Covey, 1990).

As an organization continues to focus on urgent, current, reality-based initiatives, several dynamics begin to take place. These dynamics can be characterized by the mental models that become acted out by the employees. These include: "We will never be effective if we keep changing," "How can

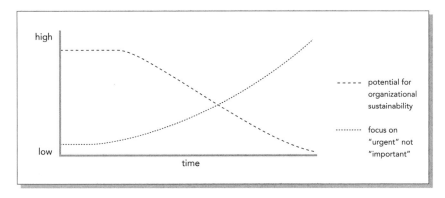

Fig 11.1 The relationship between focus and sustainability

we increase accountability with constant change?" and "Are we still headed in the same direction as we were?"

This mental model can result in a diminished ability on the part of employees to work as effectively as they can. This dynamic is not unusual. Until the late 1950s, it was a common belief that man could not run a mile in less than four minutes. When Roger Bannister broke the four-minute barrier, suddenly others began to run a mile in less than four minutes – the belief that it could not be done was broken by the evidence that it could in fact be achieved. Through an example of a successful attempt, more success became possible.

In organizations, if we begin to believe that we cannot be effective due to ongoing reorganization efforts, the end result will be reduced effectiveness. Without appropriate benchmarks of success that can be quantified and qualified, people will feel they are being put in a vicious circle of increased chaos. Effectiveness is a function of knowing where the organization is going, how it is to get there, and what part we all play in that movement. As the addiction to ongoing change increases, the potential for organizational effectiveness will decrease.

The themes seen in each case study in this book are the same: issues around the ability to see and understand the organizational vision, issues around how organizations communicate and understand, and issues around how employees think and resolve problems. These themes reflect the three core competencies – vision, understanding, and thinking systemically – necessary to have an effective organization.

Accountability in organizations is usually defined as being evaluated on what we do and how well we do it. In an organization that is undergoing constant change, it can be difficult to know what to do, and therefore how to do it. Additionally, as organizations move their employees from division to division or shuffle old employees out and new ones in, the ability to know who is to do what is diminished. As we move people from one area to another while effectiveness efforts are under way, they will develop a tendency to fall back into old ways of doing business – no rewards for effectiveness will lead to reduced effectiveness activity. Addiction to organizational change as a way to do business will decrease the potential for accountability in the organization.

An ongoing problem in many organizations is the loss of organizational "history." It is the history, or organizational memory, that can keep an organization from reliving many of the mistakes that organizations face over and over again. When the organization loses much of its capacity for retaining its history, it is not only doomed to relive the same mistakes, it can find itself being pulled and driven by both internal and external political influences. These influences have a tendency over time to change the stated direction or vision of the organization in a de facto manner. The organizational vision may remain constant, but the actions that the organization takes are in opposition to the stated vision, i.e. they are congruent with the organizational influences but not with the organizational collective knowledge. The addiction to change will decrease the ability to see and understand the long-term vision for an organization.

A result of these mental models and the actions they stimulate can be a belief on the part of senior management that the employees of an organization are not competent, nor have the capacity to help move an organization forward, resulting in less effectiveness (*see* Fig 11.2). This result will increase the addiction to constant organizational change. Addiction to reorganizational change causes increased evidence of these mental models and their subsequent actions, leading to more organizational change. The outcome can be a belief that the senior management of an organization is literally leading the change for the sake of keeping enough fluidity to reinforce their position as the only ones who can lead the organization. This is counter-productive if the organization is trying to become more sustainable over time.

The dynamics of ongoing change are relatively easy to see. The driver of change is usually a belief on the part of senior management that the organization is not as effective as it should be. The relationship between the problem symptom and the remedy is seen in Fig 11.3. In this model, the less effective an organization appears to be, the more senior management uses reorgani-

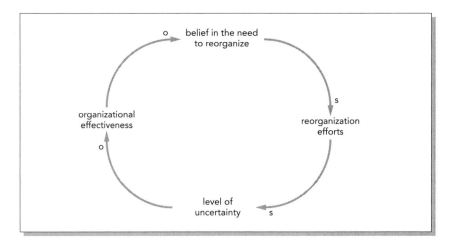

Fig 11.2 A deterioration in effectiveness

zation as a technique to remedy the situation. The model shows that as the reorganizational efforts increase, the organization should become more effective and, therefore, the less the organization should need to reorganize. Unfortunately, there is strong reason to believe that simple reorganization is a "quick-fix" remedy, and its effects may not last over time. Another option to increase organizational effectiveness can be found in Fig 11.4.

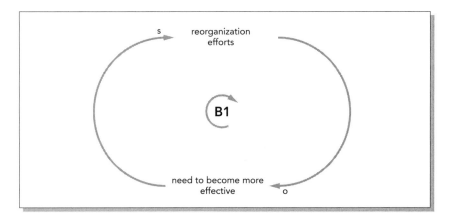

Fig 11.3 Relationship between the problem symptom and a quick-fix

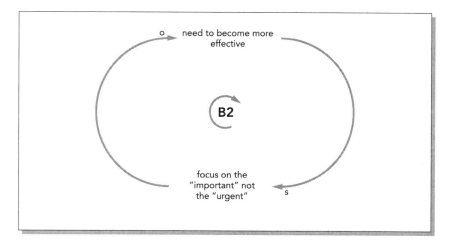

Fig 11.4 Long-term solution to a gap between the desired level of organizational effectiveness and the current reality

In Fig 11.4, a long-term solution to a gap in the desired level of organizational effectiveness and the current reality is the development of focus on initiatives that are important, not simply those that are urgent in nature. This is a key point. If initiatives are focussed on urgent organizational needs, their potential will be nil, but their impact will be great.

Focussing on initiatives that are important, and holding the organization accountable for their achievement, will act as a long-term fundamental solution, not simply another quick fix. When both these options for increasing organizational effectiveness are plotted together, the addiction dynamic becomes apparent (*see* Fig 11.5). The more senior management opts for reorganization as a method for increasing effectiveness (a short-term quick fix), the less stable the organization will be. This lack of stability can lead to the belief on the part of senior management that the employees are not capable of becoming more effective, and this will lead to a reinforcement of the belief in the need for someone who can "save" the organization.

The savior of choice of senior management is, of course, the existing senior management. If this dynamic falls into place, there would be no reason to implement "important" initiatives, for the mental model in play is that the staff competency level is low and therefore unable to differentiate between "important" and "urgent." Having few ways to actively measure

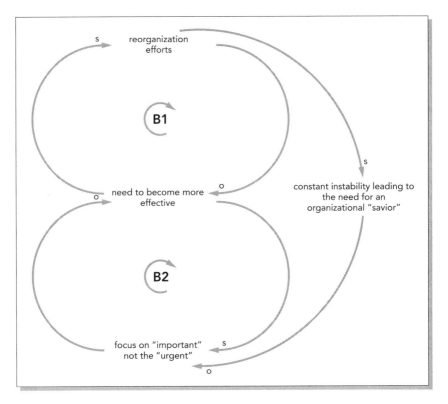

Fig 11.5 The addiction of being "saved"

effectiveness or sustainability, the organization falls back into reorganization as the technique of choice for increasing effectiveness, again providing reinforcement for the addictive behaviors of senior management. This dynamic is additionally impacted by most organizational reward systems – systems that reward today, and not tomorrow.

Organizations that have focussed on urgency as a "way to live"

TexCo

TexCo, a large energy organization that had been experiencing exponential growth in the past few years, made the decision to invoke an initiative to increase its earnings. This action was driven by perceptions both internally and externally that the earnings level could be higher due to the string of acquisitions it had made. The initiative undertaken was one to reduce spending to third parties by a fixed amount.

On the surface, the initiative was incredibly successful – the target savings were achieved and the earnings target was hit. However, the activity associated with the initiative left many negative effects that will impact the TexCo organization for many years. Additionally, the focus of the initiative was restricted to only "quick hits," savings that would be realized almost immediately. The focus on the initiative, which was admittedly "urgent," diverted attention from potential initiatives that would have enabled the company to become more effective and, therefore, sustainable over time. In lieu of effectiveness, TexCo opted for efficiency – the urgent, not the important.

EduCo

The senior management of EduCo, a large Midwest service organization, had been working for several years to increase the revenue generated by a sales division. After the most recent reorganization of the division, the newly appointed leader was given sales targets. The new leader made the decision to "invest" in her people to increase their capacity to be effective in what they were doing. This investment included training in sales techniques, but also training in organizational learning concepts and applications, and in increasing personal effectiveness. As time went on, sales targets began to be hit, but within one year, senior management became impatient and called for another reorganization. This decision, based on urgency, undermined the gains made by focussing on the important, and set the division back on both financial and organizational climate measures.

OilCo

OilCo, a medium-level player in the oil field service industry, was being inundated with problems from several areas. First, the market was taking a steep dive with the falling price of oil; second, the company's ability to consolidate several recent acquisitions was diminishing; and third, it had overrun most of its computer systems – systems that would enable it to run a new, larger company. The decision was made to drive an initiative to purchase an ERP solution to deal with these problems. On the surface, this seemed like a logical choice – acquire a new, technologically-based system that would enable the company to consolidate the acquisitions systems and help it develop better projections of how to remain viable in a fluctuating market. However, this response to multiple problems was quite myopic in its scope. The senior managers knew that they had to replace the technology systems, but they were unwilling to make the commitment to dealing with the problems that are inherent in merging multiple organizational cultures. They focussed on solving the urgent need, not the long-term, important need.

In all these case examples, several themes stand out. All the organizations, TexCo, EduCo, and OilCo, were reacting to real or perceived problems that were impacting their companies. But the way in which they dealt with them was to place their focus on the urgent, not the important problem impacts. Additionally, each organization was acting out behaviors that they had acted out before. They had become addicted to these behaviors – the behavior of reacting, not understanding and then developing fundamental, systemic solutions to problems. These addictions would result in diminished capacity to be effective and, therefore, sustainable over time.

This dynamic has been seen in each of the case studies accessed for this book. The ToolCo story showed a focus on dealing with competitive prices as opposed to solidifying an organizational brand as a way to deal with competition; the ConnectCo story demonstrated a focus on personal beliefs and the need to be right as opposed to surfacing the mental models of each participant; the OsirisCo story showed an overall concern for bottom-line dollars and productivity instead of a focus on how the organizational merger had impacted the employees' ability to be productive; and the DrillCo story surfaced an underlying belief on the part of a senior manager that chaos was good and acceptable instead of trying to learn how that chaos was impacting the organizational effectiveness.

As the addiction to "urgent-based" change initiatives grows, the mental models of the people affected by the changes tend to solidify. They include:

- it doesn't do any good to try to put forth an extra effort;
- lack of knowledge is the real key to the problem;
- constant change inhibits the potential for reorganization efforts to become effective;
- we are just reliving "quick-fix" actions of the past;
- political influences are driving the change process;
- chaos never allows real accountability to be evaluated;

● it is easier to blame than to learn;

● pitting people against each other through blame eliminates putting forth extra effort;

● questioning change efforts can be extremely risky professionally, and can result in either public humiliation, the appearance of not being of the "team," or possible termination.

The addictive dynamics of ongoing organizational change can result in several things. All will have a long-term detrimental impact on the organization and its potential over time, i.e. sustainability. This has been seen in the case study work. First, constant change creates a situation in which people rarely stay in a department or division long enough for any change efforts to take effect. This results in the loss of organizational memory, which in turn leads to reliving organizational mistakes. Without the ability to "remember" the organizational past, corporations and institutions will make costly, avoidable mistakes that can and will negatively impact both effectiveness and sustainability potential (consider ConnectCo, OsirisCo, WireCo, and GlobalCo).

> ● The addictive dynamics of ongoing organizational change can result in several things.

Second, constant organizational change sets up the belief that few in the organization have knowledge as to what the next change will be, or what the overall plan for change will be. Without a collective understanding of the "big picture," it becomes more difficult to expect the employees to work collectively to help move the organization forward to achieve its goals and vision (consider ToolCo, OsirisCo, DrillCo, WireCo, WestCo, ClassCo, and GlobalCo).

Third, in conjunction with the previous characteristic, constant organizational change helps reinforce the organizational power structure. This is due to the lack of understanding or knowledge as to the overall change direction and plan. Consequently, there is the belief that some organizational power structures keep "stirring the organizational pot" to retain organizational control and therefore retain control over the system that rewards the appearance of "constant organizational change equals effectiveness" (consider ToolCo, ConnectCo, OsirisCo, DrillCo, WireCo, WestCo, ClassCo, and GlobalCo).

Fourth, constant organizational change leads to the ability of external forces to exert political pressure on senior management that can lead to knee-jerk reactions that are not in the best interests of the long-term future of the organization, its employees, and stakeholders. Reacting to external forces can be fatal to an organization (consider ToolCo, ConnectCo, OsirisCo, DrillCo, and WestCo).

The impact of addiction to organizational change leads to behaviors that are parallel to other forms of addiction. More traditional addictions lead to feelings of worthlessness, remorse, incompetence, and the belief that everything, including the long-term future of the organization, is out of one's control. In the case of organizational addiction to change, the evident behaviors are similar.

Traditional addiction symptoms	Management/organizational symptoms
Loss of connectedness to others	Lack of support and buy-in
Feelings of worthlessness	Not adding value to organizational
Fractionalization of organizational efforts	efforts
Fear of loss of addiction	Loss of power and control
Out-of-control life patterns	Disconnection to organization
Don't care, just need the "fix"	Rapid changes

By understanding the similarities between traditional addiction symptoms and those visible in organizations, we can get a better understanding of how to deal with the addiction. Unless the addiction experienced by management is mitigating an organization's ability to be effective, organizations will continue to relive the dynamics that they have experienced in the past – lack of vision, lack of understanding, and lack of ability to think systemically.

When implementing change in organizations, senior management should consider several lessons that impact organizational effectiveness. These include:

- **Make change efforts visible** Not communicating the rationale, method, and plans for change will reduce the ability of the organization to buy in and support the change efforts. This is the main point of the core competency of vision – to ensure that everyone in an organization can "see" where the organization is trying to go in the future. This is a key element in achieving an organizational shared vision.

● **Develop clear measures of accountability** Even in the midst of change, it is crucial to enable an employee group to see how they will be held accountable for the success of the change efforts. Once again, this is an issue that relates to the core competency of vision – enabling all the organizational employees to see what will be expected of them. Additionally, this represents a direct connection to the core competency of understanding – without being able to understand what the ramifications are of actions.

● **Increase input from employees** A key element to organizational change efforts is the input from all employee levels that will be impacted by the changes. Without high levels of input, the efforts will be those only of senior management and the level of active buy-in will be reduced. This element represents an understanding of all three core competencies: vision – increased input from employees will help to ensure a collective perspective on where the organization is going; understanding – increased input from employees will promote a two-way conversation between management and employees, and therefore increase the potential for understanding in both population groups; systemic thinking – increasing input from employees can help to ensure that multiple perspectives on some of the dynamics of a proposed initiative can be surfaced.

● **Stay focussed on the organizational vision** The connection of reorganizational efforts to the organizational vision will be key to the success of the efforts and the level of organizational buy-in. Stability in focus can help to increase the likelihood that a group of employees will understand what is expected of them – core competencies of vision and understanding.

● **Be consistent in dealing with employees** When employees feel they are being treated differently than others, the organizational climate will suffer, reducing the potential for reorganizational success. Consistency, or the lack of it, has an impact on an organization's ability to be effective over time. By focussing on the core competencies, employees can better understand the dynamic relationships between consistency in messages and actions.

● **Look at the long-term ramifications of change efforts** Developing quick-fix answers to problems is easy, but developing long-term solutions to fundamental organizational problems requires an examination of both the short and long-term impact on the organization. This recommendation has a direct connection to the core competency of systemic thinking – by increasing the employees' ability to think systemically, it is easier to understand the ramifications of change efforts.

● **Make explicit the connection between any organizational initiatives and long-term organizational sustainability** When the connection between initiatives and sustainability is not made, an employee group is left with the belief that the purpose of the initiative is narrow in focus and short term in nature – a function of the core competency of understanding.

In this era of increasing competition and decreasing resources, it is crucial for organizations to become more effective and therefore sustainable. However, the methods for becoming more effective need to be examined prior to any change efforts. Senior management is traditionally held responsible for the success of organizations, and success should be measured over long periods of time, not just the next quarter. By supporting the development of the three core competencies for employees of all levels, management help to ensure that sustainability.

In my research, I have been able to utilize a series of tools that have enabled me to better understand the validity of these recommendations. These have included the Vision Deployment Matrix (VDM), Left-Hand Column (LHC), causal loop diagrams (CLDs), and systems archetypes.

The VDM, developed by Daniel Kim, is a tool that visibly shows the various dimensions of an organization. This can be valuable for an organization undergoing change. The matrix (*see* Fig 11.6) can be used for several purposes, including making change efforts visible, increasing input from employees, helping stay focussed on the organizational vision, looking at the long-term ramifications of change efforts, and making the connection between any organizational initiatives and long-term sustainability.

When facilitating the utilization of the VDM, I have found that it is very important to spend some time with the subject group ensuring that they clearly understand the definitions of terms used in the matrix. These include:

● vision – a clear picture of what an organization will look like in the future;

● mental models – the beliefs and assumptions that guide our actions, i.e. how we believe the world works;

● systemic structures – the explicit and implicit policies and procedures, the stated goals of an organization, physical layout, and the physical capacity of the organization;

	Desired future reality	Current reality	Gaps or challenges	Action steps	Indicators of progress
Vision					
Mental models What are the beliefs and assumptions that will be congruent with the vision?					
Systemic structures How can we create structures that will be consistent with those beliefs?					
Patterns What patterns of behavior do we want the structure to produce?					
Events Can we describe tangible events that would indicate the vision has been achieved?					

Fig 11.6 The Vision Deployment Matrix

● patterns of behavior – the organizational behaviors that are visible over time;

● events – the tangible, visible things that are seen in organizations;

● desired future reality – what we want the organization to look like in the future;

● current reality – what the organization looks like today;

● gaps or challenges – the difference between the desired future reality and the current reality;

● action steps – what can be done to close the gap between the future and the current realities;

● indicators of progress – the visible ways in which an organization will be able to see that the action steps have produced the desired results.

Once the subject population has a clear understanding of the terms used in the matrix, it can be effective to begin by asking individuals to fill out the first two vertical columns (desired future reality and current reality). This should be done individually as it is an opportunity for the participants to begin to articulate their perceptions and beliefs of the organization, both now and in the future. Upon completion, it can be very effective to then have relatively small groups – of three to four people – of the subject population share their views as they have written them. The purpose of this "sharing" of perceptions is to begin to build a shared view of the organization, both in the current reality and in the desired future reality.

This is an iterative process, with the number of times that it is done depending on the size of the population group being facilitated. At each step of the process, there is a gain in the level of shared vision regarding the current organizational reality and the desired future organizational reality. This is facilitated through conversations before, during, and after completion of each version level. Upon completion of a "final" or collective view by the employees that are being worked with, an additional conversation is held with the entire group to ensure that there is alignment with what the cells in the first two columns of the matrix state. At this point in the process, the balance of the matrix can be filled out, either by the entire group with the use of a facilitator, or by a smaller, representative group.

> ● The Vision Deployment Matrix can help an organization and its employees look at the current and long-term ramifications of organizational change efforts or ineffectiveness on multiple levels.

My experiences with the use of the matrix have shown me that the benefits of the completed matrix process are worth the effort put in. I have used the VDM with employee groups that are undergoing large-scale change efforts, populations that have been quite stable but largely ineffective, and populations that are a combination of both situations (*see* Fig 11.7).

The Vision Deployment Matrix can help an organization and its employees look at the current and long-term ramifications of organizational change efforts or ineffectiveness on multiple levels, including the structural level, the pattern of behaviors level, the event level, and the mental models level. Additionally, the development of the matrix by employees helps to

	Desired future reality	Current reality	Gaps or challenges	Action steps	Indicators of progress
Vision To be the premier multi-discipline consulting firm to assist clients in managing risk.	• Premier firm in valued risk solutions • All employees are committed to goals • Integrated service line	• Silo service line • Vision continuously revised • A leader but in chosen markets	• Vision not fully articulated • Lack of understanding and integration	• Develop consensus on vision • Communicate vision on regular basis	• Number of people who know and understand vision
Mental models What are the beliefs and assumptions that will be congruent with the vision?	• Open to learning • No fear of failure • Productivity is important	• Lack of EE trust • Reactive • "I" vs. "We"	• Believe that investment in HR is a return • Building environment that fosters EE trust • Lack of openness to change	• Term building and learning sessions • Develop improvement programs and processes • Conduct forecasting meetings	• Attendance of learning sessions • Employee surveys
Systemic structures How can we create structures that will be consistent with those beliefs?	• Flat organization • Performance measures aligned with vision • Formal knowledge sharing	• Hierarchical • Isolated knowledge sharing practices • PM are short term and financially driven	• Silo structure • PM not aligned with vision • PM promotes self-interest	• Create training database • Develop PM's aligned with long-term goals • Develop uniform methodology	• PM's changed • Number of integrated projects sold • Populated and updated "knowledge" base
Patterns What patterns of behavior do we want the structure to produce?	• Integrated efforts among business units • Better retention rates	• Training not fully supported • Ad hoc knowledge sharing • Competition among business units • Turnover	• No follow through on ideas or integrated effort • Lack of empowerment • Broken training curriculum	• Accept work aligned with vision • Teams pitch proposals together • "Shock treatment"	• Higher retention rates • Increased investment and return on training
Events Can we describe tangible events that would indicate the vision has been achieved	• Fastest growing service line • Increased training • Increased market recognition	• Growth in personnel • Crisis management • Increase in number of risk engagements	• Lack of personnel (skilled and trained) • Integrated projects not sold • No proactive marketing	• Training programs • Identify reasons for leaving and correct • Build skills inventory	• Increased net revenue • Increased client satisfaction

PM = Performance Measure
EE = Employee

Fig 11.7 The Vision Deployment Matrix in use

increase their involvement in the process of change. These benefits reinforce the importance of the core competencies of vision, understanding, and systemic thinking as it is these three competencies that enable the employees to fill in the matrix.

Left-Hand Column can be used effectively when there are underlying issues in an organization that are hard to surface or when the employees believe there are implicit meanings behind actions. The utilization of Left-Hand Column can help surface the issues behind change efforts, help understand the rationale behind accountability measures, improve consistency in dealing with employees, and help to understand the relationship between organizational initiatives and long-term organizational sustainability. The LHC is especially effective in an organization that has multiple undiscussable issues that appear to plague progress over time.

In my research and work, I have used the LHC both informally and formally. Informally, I have asked various people what they believe are the undiscussable issues facing their organizations. After hearing their responses, I have then inquired as to why those issues appear to be undiscussable – what is behind the inability to discuss them. On a formal basis, I have used the LHC with an organization when it has become apparent that there is a disconnection between what is being said by senior management, and what the balance of the organization believes is being said.

One example was an institution of higher education in the Midwest. In this large organization, it was apparent that there was this disconnection – a variance between what was being said and what was being heard. The concern was that the disconnection was undiscussable in the organization. To surface this, I identified a group (of eight people) who were willing to participate in an experiment with the Left-Hand Column tool. At a presentation by the chief executive of the organization, the group were each given paper forms that had been divided into two columns. In the right-hand column were various excerpts from the CEO's presentation, obtained from the CEO prior to the delivery of the presentation. The left-hand column was left blank. At the point in which the CEO reached each of the excerpts, the members of the group wrote down in the left-hand column what they thought was behind those statements. The information they wrote included what they thought the CEO really meant if they believed that the statement could not be taken at face value. At the end of the presentation, the group met to share what they had written in their LHC forms. This information was then used to build a collective left-hand column of the presentation, which was subsequently supplied to the CEO as feedback.

Several facts emerged from this. First, it was apparent that the CEO was not aware that the population he was speaking to was interpreting what was said in multiple ways. Second, it was apparent to the group that the CEO had several unstated agendas that he was trying to push through the organization. And third, it was apparent that until that day, both of these perceptions could not be discussed within the organization.

By using the Left-Hand Column tool, it was possible to surface these undiscussables and move the organization past them. This was possible by utilizing the input from the employees of the organization, an effective utilization of the core competency of understanding. Additionally, the utilization of this tool was an effective utilization of the core competency of systemic thinking by helping to illuminate some of the dynamics at play in the organization (*see* Fig 11.8).

What I am thinking	**What was said**
His positive examples referenced "he," not "we." Aren't we all in this together?	"I am struggling with all of these problems. It is hard work, but it is important to our long-term future here at (institutional name)."
He says positions, but all he will really do is just put the positions on hold for ever. We might as well have lost them if he locks them up in limbo.	"There will be no loss in positions."
He may have said that these issues need to be resolved, but then he tells everyone what he has done about them. Is this getting our input or just trying to let us think that we will have input when all that will happen is that he will get his way after all?	"Here are some policy issues that need to be resolved."
If things are so clear, why wouldn't people understand? If we ask questions, we will be made to look stupid or feel stupid. Who wants that to happen? No thank you.	"You need to ask questions if you don't understand what I am talking about."

Fig 11.8 Dynamics at play

At a time when organizations appear to be focussing on how to make more money to support "next quarter's earnings" data, the issue of sustainability may not seem to be important. For an organization that appears to be focussing on initiatives that are urgent in nature – urgency is defined as a focus on an extremely short time frame, one quarter at a time – the impact of core competencies on the dynamics of organizational change may not seem to be important either. However, my research has led me to believe that it is the core competencies, or more importantly, the effective utilization of core competencies, that may prove to be a key element in the ability of an organization to be sustainable over time.

Through the implementation and utilization of core competencies as a way for an organization to learn how to become more effective, the organization can produce several "wins." Through the utilization of the competencies of vision, understanding, and systemic thinking, employees can achieve a better understanding of what it takes to make an organization more effective, what it takes to make an organization sustainable, and what it takes for them to contribute to these organizational gains.

At a time when organizations appear to be demonstrating very short-term thinking, the long-term sustainability and effectiveness of organizations are at risk. The utilization of core competencies, most specifically vision, understanding, and systemic thinking, is becoming more critical. In all the case studies that were developed for the purposes of this book, it is the distinct lack of utilization of these core competencies that is impacting the organizations' ability to deal effectively with the issues confronting them. By shifting their focus from short-term thinking to a long-term concentration on sustainability, the organizations can enhance their ability to be effective over time. To enable this shift in focus, each of the organizations will need to utilize the core competencies of vision, understanding, and systemic thinking.

Causal loop diagrams and systems archetypes are especially useful when employees are having a hard time "seeing" the interrelationships between actions and outcomes. This can help to make change efforts visible, show the implications of accountability measures, increase input from organizational employees, keep the organizational vision in front of employees, provide clarity regarding the long-term ramifications of change efforts, and make visible the connection between organizational initiatives and long-term organizational sustainability issues. Throughout this book, I have utilized causal loop diagrams and systems archetypes to illuminate some of the dynamics that I have learned during my research.

When asked what the principal assets of an organization are, the typical CEO might well answer, "the people." But when asked further about how the organization shows this asset on its financial statements, most CEOs will begin to mumble about the relative inflexibility of its accounting system. Is this an indicator of accounting's inflexibility or of the pervasive mental models that abound that people *cost* our organizations money? The foundations of this mental model could be built on the belief that people are valued when they have specific, explicit skills. This belief pattern is changing in the world of business.

However, this belief pattern is complicated by our beliefs about people and what they can bring to an organization. Many senior managers are convinced that the best people to have working for them are ones with high-level degrees from recognized universities. Many others believe that it is key to have employees that have years of hands-on experience in a specific field. Others believe that solely having enough employees is the key to success. Think of the questions that you were asked when you were last interviewed for a job. In most cases, the questions revolved around education and experience. How many people did you manage? How many dollars did you manage? How much profit did your efforts generate for the organization? These could all be very relevant, and in most organizations they apparently are. But the key question that we fail to ask potential employees is, "What are the core skills that you can bring to our organization?" This question is usually missing, as most senior managers have not gained an understanding of what core skills can truly add value to an organization. These core skills will be especially important due to the pervasive increase in the level of global competition, the compression of available transaction time for our organizations, and the increasingly difficult ability to keep our organizations sustainable over time.

There are three core skills that each employee of the organization of the year 2000 and beyond will need to have if they are to truly add value to an organization. They are vision, understanding, and the ability to think systemically.

Vision

Vision, as defined by most people, is the ability to see a future condition that is different than the current reality being faced. Vision is a way of describing the future condition. Having the ability to develop and communicate a vision is a precursor to being able to develop a shared vision, and shared vision is a necessary discipline for employees who wish to become more sustainable over time. Without a visible, clearly defined future condition or vision, it is rare that an employee group is able to move forward collectively. This usually results in fragmented efforts, wasted resources, and varying states of organizational entropy. A clearly defined organizational vision is a way in which to build in alignment, not only for where an organization needs to go in the future but for the vehicle that can stimulate effective planning efforts to move the organization forward.

Understanding

The core capability of understanding is a key to the positive movement of an organization. Understanding refers to the ability to listen empathically. This does not mean solely listening to what is being said or what is printed; it refers to the ability to hear not only the words but also the meaning behind the words.

Understanding is necessary if an organization is to move collectively toward a future state in alignment. Without understanding, the organizational efforts will be fragmented, resulting in various employees moving in different directions. This will absorb valuable organizational resources. Without the ability to understand, it is hard to conceive how we can expect to be in alignment with the key issues and challenges facing our organizations today.

Thinking systemically

Thinking in wholes is the systems thinking piece of the core capabilities. Thinking in wholes is a way to describe how we see the dynamics that are present in our organizations. For years, we have been taught that to be effective, we need to be able to understand the component elements of our organizations. We have also been encouraged to increase the effectiveness of our component organizational elements. This has resulted in two types of thinking: mechanistic thinking and binary thinking. Mechanistic thinking is the belief that in order to understand a complex organization we must mentally "break" the organization into small, understandable pieces. This if fine if we want to explore how an organization is put together, but it is not an effective way in which to explore how an organization functions. Organizations are more than just collections of components; they are components that interact in certain ways (*see* Fig 11.9).

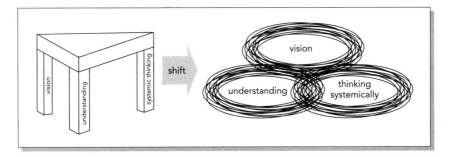

Fig 11.9

To explore how the organization functions, the dynamics at play within it, we must look at the interrelationships that are present in the organization. Take the analogy of a fine watch. To understand how a watch functions, it needs more than just taking the watch apart and measuring all the gears and levers. It becomes apparent when doing this that what you have is merely a collection of gears and levers in front of you. This is not a watch, nor will it function as a watch. To understand the watch and how it functions, one must examine the interrelationships of the components of the watch. This can only be done while the watch is working, i.e. all the components working together.

Binary thinking is the result of years of being taught that, to be effective, we have to have the "right" answer. This is a concept that is taught and rewarded in schools. Those who have the "right" answer succeed; those who do not, fail. This concept has not been lost on adults who are desperately trying to improve the effectiveness of their organizations. The drawback to binary thinking is that, if there is a "right" answer, then all other answers are wrong. Working to improve the effectiveness of organizations is not the same as mathematics. There are no singularly right answers. In organizations, there are many ways in which to improve; some are proven to be clearly better than others. This does not make them "right," it only means that they worked. There could be other answers that could have been better, more effective solutions to the problems facing the organization.

Originally thought to be rather static, and consequently drawn as a three-legged stool with each leg needed to support the idea of the competencies, we have begun to shift our thinking by learning that the relationship between them is in reality quite dynamic in nature. Many senior managers would still like us to believe that the most effective way to improve their employees' level of competence is to focus on explicit training areas, i.e. technology training.

These capabilities focus on tacit knowledge. Most training programs are targetted to improve the explicit knowledge levels of those who participate in the training. In most cases, this includes specific technical skills. For a computer programer, this could include how computer programs function, how to write programs, how to de-bug programs, etc. For a customer service representative, the technical skills might include how and where to find answers to customers' concerns, how to track customer follow-up, etc. For a marketing person, these skills could include how to determine market potential, how to develop marketing strategies, how to develop marketing vehicles, etc. These are all skills that focus on explicit knowledge, the "how" to do our jobs.

To be effective over time, an organization must ensure that its population has more than just explicit skills. Organizations need to have tacit skills, the "why" of how to do the job. It is through enhancing the core capabilities of a group of employees that the organization can realize its potential by ensuring that the population has the ability to develop personal and shared visions, to understand, and to think in wholes.

We are coming to learn that if an employee does not have high levels of these three core competencies, he or she will not be able to effectively utilize the explicit skills. Explicit skills are of use only when an employee knows how and why the organization needs them – vision. Explicit skills are of use only when an employee understands the rationale behind them and their impact on the organization – understanding. Explicit skills are of use only when an employee understands the dynamic relationships at play in the organization and how the skills will enhance overall organizational sustainability – systemic thinking. It is these three core competencies, these tacit skills, that can provide the highest leverage for organizational growth over time.

The benefits of focussing on core competencies

By helping to enhance the core capabilities of employees of all levels, the organization can set a direction that says several things. First, enabling employees to enhance their core capabilities shows a commitment to investing in people. This investment can pay off by increasing the likelihood that employees will be able to realize their personal potential – increasing personal effectiveness will lead to client satisfaction and organizational success (*see* loop R1 in Fig 11.10).

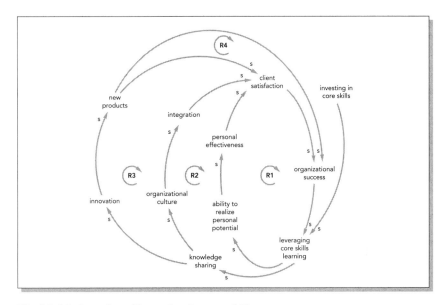

Fig 11.10 Benefits of investing in core skills

Second, working to enhance the core skill capabilities of an employee population increases the level of knowledge sharing, improving an organizational culture and the level of integration of organizational efforts. This, too, leads to higher levels of client satisfaction and organizational success (loop R2).

Third, by focussing on the core capabilities of its people, the organization's ability to innovate increases. This can result in new products, satisfying the demand from current and potential clients, and thus increasing organizational success (loop R3).

Fourth, through the development of new products and services, the organization increases its potential to develop new revenue streams, again increasing organizational success (loop R4).

The core capabilities of vision, understanding, and thinking in wholes are the key to organizational learning. By enhancing these core capabilities, employees can achieve their potential and that of the organization itself. It is the core capabilities of vision, understanding, and thinking systemically that are the foundation for organizational effectiveness.

Bibliography

Argyris, Chris (1990) *Overcoming Organizational Defenses*, Needham Heights, MA: Allyn and Bacon.

Argyris, Chris and Schon, Donald (1992) *Theory in Practice: Increasing Professional Effectiveness*, Jossey-Bass.

Augustine, Norman R. (1997) "Reshaping an industry: Lockheed Martin's survival story," *Harvard Business Review*, Volume 75, Number 3, 83–94.

Barks, Coleman and Moyne, John (1995) *The Essential Rumi*, San Francisco: Harper.

Beckhard, Richard and Harris, Reuben T. (1987) *Organizational Transitions*. Addison-Wesley.

Block, Peter (1981) *Flawless Consulting*, Pfeiffer.

Blohowiak, Donald (1996) "After the downsizing: building a resilient organization in a radical change environment," *National Productivity Review*, Volume 16, Number 1, 3–6.

Bohm, David (1985) *Unfolding Meaning*, London: Routledge.

Bridges, William (1991) *Managing Transitions*, Perseus.

Brunner, Jerome (1996) *The Culture of Education*, Cambridge, MA: Harvard University Press.

Bryner, Andy and Markova, Dawna (1996) *An Unused Intelligence*, Berkeley, CA: Conari Press.

Brynjolfsson, Erik, Austin Renshaw, Amy and Alstyne, Marshall Val (1997) "The matrix of change," *Sloan Management Review*, Volume 38, Number 2, 37–54.

Buxton, Jayne and Davidson, Mike (1996) "Building a sustainable growth capability," *Strategy and Leadership*, Volume 24, Number 6, 32–38.

Chakravarthy, Bala (1997) "A new strategy framework for coping with turbulence," *Sloan Management Review*, Volume 38, Number 2, 69–82.

Collins, James C. and Porras, Jerry I. (1991) "Organizational vision and visionary organizations," *California Management Review*, Volume 34, Number 1, 30–52.

Conner, Daryl (1993) *Managing at the Speed of Change*. Villard.

Covey, Stephen (1989) *The 7 Habits of Highly Effective People*, New York: Fireside.

Covey, Stephen (1990) *Principle Centered Leadership*, New York: Summit.

Davis, Brian, *et al.* (1996) *Successful Manager's Handbook*, Minneapolis: Personal Decisions International.

Day, George S. (1997) "Strategies for surviving a shakeout," *Harvard Business Review*, Volume 75, Number 2, 92–102.

De Geus, Arie (1997) *The Living Company*, Cambridge, MA: Harvard Business School Press.

Fisher, James and Tack, Martha (1988) *Leaders on Leadership: The College Presidency*, San Francisco: Jossey-Bass.

Fritz, Robert (1984) *The Path of Least Resistance*, New York: Fawcett.

Fritz, Robert (1996) *Corporate Tides*, San Francisco: Berret-Koehler.

Gallwey, Timothy (1974) *The Inner Game of Tennis*, New York: Random House.

Gardner, Howard (1983) *Frames of Mind*, New York: Basic.

Gardner, John, *et al.* (1995) *Community Building in Business*, San Francisco: New Leaders Press.

Garvin, David A. (1993) "Building a learning organization," *Harvard Business Review*, Volume 71, Number 4, 78–91.

Gyatso, Tenzin (1995) *The World of Tibetan Buddhism*, Boston: Wisdom.

Halal, William E. (1997) "Creating an entrepreneurial university: toward a democratic marketplace of ideas," *On The Horizon*, Volume 5, Number 2, 1–6.

Heifetz, Ronald A. and Laurie, Donald L. (1997) "The work of leadership," *Harvard Business Review*, Volume 75, Number 1, 124–134.

Huntington, Samuel (1996) *The Clash of Civilizations and the Remaking of the World Order*, New York. Simon & Schuster.

Hurst, David K. (1997) "When it comes to real change, too much objectivity may be fatal to the process," *Strategy & Leadership*, Volume 25, Number 2, 6–12.

Issacs, William (1993) "Dialogue: the power of collective thinking," *The Systems Thinker*, Volume 4, Number 3, 1–4.

Jaworski, Joseph (1996) *Synchronicity*, San Francisco: Berrett-Koehler.

Jick, Todd (1992) *Managing Change*, Harvard Business School Press.

Jung, C. G. (1973) *Synchronicity*, Princeton, NJ: Princeton University Press.

Kanter, Rosabeth Moss (1992) "Moving ideas into action: mastering the art of Change," *Harvard Business Review*, 10 October.

Kanter, Rosabeth Moss, Stein, Barry and Jick, Todd (1992) *The Challenge of Organizational Change*, New York: Free Press/Macmillan.

Kelly, Kevin (1994) *Out of Control*, Reading, PA: Addison-Wesley.

Kim, Daniel (1993) "The link between individual and organizational learning," *Sloan Management Review*, Volume 35, Number 1, 37–50.

Kim, Daniel (1993) "A framework and methodology for linking individual and organizational learning: applications in TQM and product development," Diss. MIT.

Kleiner, Art (1996) *The Age of Heretics*, New York: Currency Doubleday.

Kleiner, Art and Roth, George (1997) "How to make experience your company's best teacher," *Harvard Business Review*, Volume 75, Number 5, 172–177.

Kornfield, Jack (1993) *A Path With Heart*, New York: Bantam.

Kotter, John P. (1995) "Leading change: why transformation efforts fail," *Harvard Business Review*, March–April.

Krishnamurti, Jidduh (1964) *Think on These Things*, New York: Harper & Row.

Krishnamurti, Jidduh (1972) *You Are the World*, New York: Harper & Row.

Lakoff, George and Johnson, Mark (1980) *Metaphors We Live By*, Chicago: University of Chicago Press.

de Laszlo, Violet (ed) (1990) *The Basic Writings of C. G. Jung*, Princeton, NJ: Princeton University Press.

Lazerson, Marvin (1997) "Who owns higher education? The changing face of governance," *Change*, Volume 29, Number 2, 10–15.

Lee, Blaine (1997) *The Power of Principle*, New York: Simon & Schuster.

Lincoln, James R. (1989) "Employee work attitudes and management practice in the U.S. and Japan: Evidence from a large comparative survey," *California Management Review*, Volume 32, Number 1, 89–106.

Manzoni, Jean-Francois and Barsoux, Jean-Louis (1998) "The set-up-to-fail syndrome," *Harvard Business Review*, Volume 76, Number 2, 101–113.

Marquart, Michael and Reynolds, Angus (1994) *The Global Learning Organization*, Burr Ridge, IL: Irwin.

Morrison, James (1997) "Transforming educational organizations," *On The Horizon*, Volume 5, Number 1, 2–3.

Ober, Steven, Yanovitz, Joel and Kantor, David (1995) "Creating business results through team learning," *The Systems Thinker*, Volume 6, Number 5, 1–5.

Parker, Marjorie (1990) *Creating Shared Vision*, Oslo: Marjorie Parker.

Pinchot, Gifford and Pinchot, Elizabeth (1997) "Organizations that encourage integrity," *Journal for Quality and Productivity*, Volume 20, Number 2, 10–19.

Pritchett, Price (1997) "Overcome resistance," *Executive Excellence*, Volume 14, Number 2, 13–14.

Rieley, James (1997) "Creating practice fields," *The Systems Thinker*, Pegasus: Waltham, MA. Volume 8, Number 7, September.

Rieley, James, Soderquist, Chris and Rieley, Melissa (1998) "Using systems dynamics to enhance the learning potential of dyslexics," *The Creative Learning Exchange*, The Creative Learning Exchange: Action, MA. Volume 7, Number 1, Winter.

Rieley, James (1998) "Measuring organizational alignment," *The Systems Thinking in Action Conference Proceedings*, San Francisco, CA. September.

Rieley, James and Agatstein, Kevin (1998) "Using simulation to improve the decision-making process," *National Productivity Review*, John Wiley & Sons: New York, Winter.

Rieley, James and Leahy, Charles (1998) "Understanding the impact of a corporate buy-out," *National Productivity Review*, John Wiley & Sons: New York, Fall.

Rieley, James (1999) "Organizational exponential growth," *National Productivity Review*, John Wiley & Sons: New York, Fall.

Rieley, James and Cross, Rob (1999) "Team learning: best practices and tools for an elusive concept," *National Productivity Review*, John Wiley & Sons: New York, Summer.

Rieley, James and Rieley, Mary Lee (1999) "Is your organisation addicted to change?" *National Productivity Review*, John Wiley & Sons: New York, Summer.

Rieley, James and Agatstein, Kevin (2000) "The Rise and Fall of a 'favourite child' business unit at a major consulting firm," *Journal of Organizational Excellence*, John Wiley & Sons: New York, Winter.

Scheetz, Mary (1998) "Systems thinking and systems dynamics in K-12 education," *The Creative Learning Exchange*, Volume 7, Number 2, 7–9.

Schein, Edgar H. (1999) *The Corporate Culture Survival Guide*, Jossey-Bass.

Schwartz, Hillel (1990) *Century's End*, New York: Currency Doubleday.

Schwartz, Peter (1991) *The Art of the Long View*, New York: Currency Doubleday.

Senge, Peter (1990) *The Fifth Discipline: The Art and Practice of the Learning Organization*, New York: Doubleday.

Senge, Peter (1997) "Creating learning communities," *Executive Excellence*, Volume 14, Number 3, 17–18.

Shah, Idries (1968) *Caravan of Dreams*, London: Octagon.

Shah, Idries (1968) *The Way of the Sufi*, London: Arkana.

Smith, Douglas K. (1997) *Taking Charge of Change*, Perseus.

Tichy, Noel and Devanna, Mary Ann (1997) *The Transformational Leader*, John Wiley & Sons.

Tornow, Walter W. (1997) "Service quality and organizational effectiveness," *Human Resources Planning*, Volume 14, Number 2, 86–97.

Tornow, Walter W. and Wiley, Jack W. (1997) "Service quality and management practices: a look at employee attitudes, customer satisfaction, and bottom-line consequences," *Human Resource Planning*, Volume 14, Number 2, 105–115.

Wallace, Thomas (1994) *World Class Manufacturing*, Essex Junction, VT: Oliver Wight.

Wardman, Kellie (ed) (1994) *Reflections on Creating Learning Organizations*, Cambridge, MA: Pegasus.

Weisbord, Marvin (1992) *Discovering Common Ground*, San Francisco: Berret-Koehler.

Wheatley, Margaret J. and Kellner-Rogers, Myron (1995) "Breathing life into organizations," *Journal for Quality and Participation*, Volume 18, Number 4, 6–9.

Whyte, W. F. and Hamilton, E. L. (1961) *Action Research for Management*, Homewood, IL: Irwin-Dorsey.

Youngblood, Mark D. (1997) "Leadership at the edge of chaos: from control to creativity," *Strategy and Leadership*, Volume 25, Number 5, 8–14.

Index